Praise for *What You Become in Flight*

"Revelatory, honest, and wondrous. This is a story of constant becoming. Ellen O'Connell Whittet shows us how to confront heartbreaking realities while remaining open. She teaches us the importance of paying homage to our past selves while growing. *What You Become in Flight* is about the power we harness when we let our losses inform us. I come away in celebration of life's nonlinear path and the ways we struggle and learn to occupy our bodies."
—CHANEL MILLER, author of *Know My Name*

"I admire Ellen's care in chronicling loss, the body, movement, pain. Her writing is wide awake—prose that holds on as a mechanism for taking flight. Writing that comes up against our fears; that carries out a beautiful working through"
—DURGA CHEW-BOSE, author of *Too Much and Not the Mood*

"Piercing and poetic, Ellen O'Connell Whittet's memoir explores what happens when we lose a dream we feel like we were destined for. It is much more than a memoir about ballet; it is a memoir about being a woman with a body, about being a person with a hungry heart, someone searching for a place to belong. Whittet writes with astounding vulnerability and grace."
—ANNIE HARTNETT, author of *Rabbit Cake*

"An elegant and compelling *künstlerroman* that begins in the body and ends on the page."
—MELISSA FEBOS, author of *Whip Smart*

"Ellen O'Connell Whittet's *What You Become in Flight* is an enthralling, smart, inspiring debut. As a serious ballet dancer, Whittet takes us to the limits of what she inflicts upon her own body, and then investigates the love, violence, fear and obsession that other people inflict upon her, both on and off stage. Here, we're taken deep into the world of professional ballet, the grace, the broken bones, all at the hands of an acute observer willing to deftly marry the exquisite and grotesque. But Whittet's story is much more than a ballerina's tale. She guides us through phobias, violence's many forms, and the tales of other women in her family who form touchstones as her life unfolds into and then out of ballet, through relationships, passions, illnesses, and the biggest questions about what gives us the astonishing grace and strength required for everyday living. This is a beautiful book."
—TESSA FONTAINE, author of *The Electric Woman: A Memoir in Death-Defying Acts*

"Illuminating and lyrical. Fierce and delicate. Raw and romantic. *What You Become in Flight* is a true work of art; a contradiction of soft and rough, the grey area between black and white. This is a book not just for dancers, and not only for women. Rather, it's a gorgeous lesson to consume, leaving you full of the complex feeling of what it is to be lifted high, dropped hard, and then build yourself back up. Ellen O'Connell Whittet's words will seep deep into you, fill your head with music, heart with empathy, and, ultimately allow you to understand what it is like to have had wings."
—MIRA PTACIN, author of *The In-Betweens: The Spiritualists, Mediums, and Legends of Camp Etna*

WHAT YOU BECOME IN FLIGHT

WHAT YOU BECOME IN FLIGHT

A MEMOIR

ELLEN O'CONNELL WHITTET

What You Become in Flight

First published in 2020 by Melville House
Copyright © Ellen O'Connell Whittet
First Melville House Printing: April 2020

Melville House Publishing
46 John Street
Brooklyn, NY 11201
and
Melville House UK
Suite 2000
16/18 Woodford Road
London E7 oHA

mhpbooks.com
@melvillehouse

ISBN: 978-1-61219-832-3
ISBN: 978-1-61219-833-0 (eBook)

Library of Congress Control Number: 2019957459

Designed by Betty Lew

Printed in the United States of America
1 2 3 4 5 6 7 8 9 10

A catalog record for this book is available
from the Library of Congress

For my mother and father

"Ballet is woman."

—GEORGE BALANCHINE

"Well, it's a woman made by a man."

—PAM TANOWITZ

Contents

WHAT YOU BECOME IN FLIGHT

Prologue

It all begins with ballet.

It was nighttime, late winter in California, and I was nineteen years old. That was the winter I decided to stop eating, and began to be noticed.

The ballet we were rehearsing was called *Serenade*, and I danced it with a tall blond named Peter, who could watch choreography once and memorize exactly what he had to do. It was the kind of ballet I was perfect for, without Martha Graham contractions or Balanchine pirouettes. It was rigid, restrained, correct, viciously classical—a piece that could have been danced in France or Russia in the 1850s. It was something that my grandmother could have seen as a young woman, a way of time-traveling through centuries to watch prima ballerina Marie Taglioni dressed as the sylphide in Victor Hugo's Paris, clad in white tulle and illuminated by gas lamps.

"You run over to me and I'll do the rest," Peter had said to me. "Just leave it to me." Off to the side of the mirrored studio, I stood in black stirrup tights and pointe shoes and waited. Peter was the poet and I was the muse, appealing to his melancholic nature as a Romantic-era hero. Although my dance held his attention, I existed for his character arc, not my own.

As the piece began, he crossed the stage in a diagonal, walking, reaching, uncoiling from spinning pirouettes into arabesques, landing from the turn with his leg extended behind him in the air. The light string music suggested the quiet regularity of rain just outside. I could almost hum along to it.

I ran forward and stopped, doing the steps Peter was dancing just behind me a few counts before he did them. Peter was close by but didn't quite touch me unless I leaned so far that he needed to catch me, or I turned so much that his hands would stop my waist, spinning me until I unfolded and caught the music with my body. Though witness to each other, our steps were not the same. Mine were a prologue to his. We were two birds flying next to each other, plunging in a compact series, never wandering apart, or varying our distance from each other, but keeping our place in the sky.

"Stage right!" The choreographer directed. "Downstage! Look at her. Keep your eyes on him as he runs from you. Now run to him."

As a child, I had felt such joy and freedom when I danced, my limbs loose and always in the habit of pulling up and turning out. Dancing let me say something before I was any good at using words. That night in the studio, I tried to remember that, even though these days there was a tug in my hip flexor and a leg warmer wrapped around my tired left ankle.

I followed the choreographer's instructions, running on the balls of my pointe shoes. Running in ballet is more like skimming the surface of the stage, the arms still positioned with care, the chest leading. We had been rehearsing this scene all evening, a loop of runs and leaps, and I was feeling tired. Though he didn't look it, Peter, who had been catching me all night, was also likely exhausted. Still, I ran to him, pushing for energy that would allow me to skitter toward a man who was supposed to catch and lift me.

There was one lift I spent the whole first half of the piece dreading, and the second half giddy from remembering. The lift began with me running toward him, and when he caught me he'd flip me over one shoulder, behind his neck, and I came down over the other shoulder. When the lift went well, we looked at each other afterwards—each of us miracles who had thrown ourselves headlong into a piece of choreography, caring only that we didn't fall behind the music.

"That was my fault," he said to the choreographer when it didn't go as well. He took the blame each time.

This time I came down clumsily, still half caught in his arms. The choreographer stopped the music, and as her back was turned, Peter said to me, "Make sure your rib cage is facing me so I can get my arm underneath and grab you."

He made a swinging motion with his arms, and I understood that I was the invisible shape he was cradling in his gesture. Time and time again, when a lift went wrong, or our timing was not matched, he called the fault his and then privately told me what I should do differently. We rehearsed together after daily classes, when we were sweaty from grand allegro and warmed up enough to try the lift full out. It required him to catch me in mid-step, lift me upside down and backward all at once. When I was first learning the steps, I would watch videos of other girls who executed it perfectly—the absolute trust they had in their bodies to mold improbably with the male dancer and create a complementary moving shape. I had never been lifted upside down and backwards all at once before, and I did not know that it took two people to let one fall.

In our rehearsal, we did the steps that led me to him. He ran away, he looked back, I ran to him. I would then jump, and he would stop and catch me. That's what was supposed to happen.

And like we had rehearsed so many times, I ran toward him and jumped only to watch him as he continued forward, not stopping, leaving me behind, mid-flight. And then I was falling, a low moving kite of music and bones, of hitched breath.

I held my breath during that moment when I had no control over our movement: everything was up to Peter and the ballet and all the training I had ever had. And the floor grew and grew until my straight arm hit it, then legs, and my hip that jutted from my black tights like some rare bird. As I rolled onto my back, I felt a fate worse than gravity.

❧

An essential measure of trust is allowing someone else to carry you. When dancers give ourselves over to gravity, whether in a leap, or falling backwards, or collapsing down on ourselves or a partner, we come to depend that someone will catch us, bringing us safely back to earth. Trust in the choreographer and other dancers in rehearsals and onstage allows abandon. When we dance in tandem, we trust the movements of the other dancer to ensure we won't crash into one another, and use that trust to push our bravery, committing to the fullest expression of our movement. Dancing requires peripheral vision, but also builds a sixth sense of instinct, so we see each other not with our eyes, but with our own radiating bodies. We learn to read each other until we can predict what another dancer's body will do just by the taut quivering of a single coiled muscle. Though rehearsals began in a fluorescent-lit studio, when we performed, we took our places in the dark and once the lights rose, we often couldn't see as we hurtled ourselves towards our partners, who waited in the dark wings. The lights onstage can be disorienting, dizzying, so we had to trust our other dancers to be where we needed them to be.

In 2005, then-soloist at American Ballet Theatre Michele Wiles was making her debut in the ballet *Sylvia* when her partner lost control and dropped her from an overhead lift. "We fell flat on our faces," Wiles told *The Washington Post*. "There's no blame. Maybe just a lack of rehearsal." Being underprepared affects the level of freedom dancers allow themselves and each other onstage, certainly. But in my case that breach of trust came during a rehearsal, when we should have been more attentive to our exhaustion and limits, and more highly attuned to each other's voltage. Not all falls are catastrophic, but all of them could have been prevented. Risks in choreography are calculated—the overhead lift, for example, requires partners in a pas de deux to figure out exactly where each holds the other, where each lands, so that the audience can see the elegance rather than the danger of the choreography.

German contemporary dancer and choreographer Pina Bausch asked her dancers to trust each other and the art on stage through extremes. In "The Fall Dance," a woman falls forward repeatedly, her partner catching her mere inches from the pavement. The dance is an articulation of catch and release, of surrender and salvation, creating unrestraint and at the same time, parsing it. Watching that woman fall is like watching both a beginning and an ending in the same instant. I cannot help but watch it through my fingers, a horror film of possibility. In "Café Müller," another one of Bausch's famous pieces, the dancers make their way through a room full of chairs with their eyes closed, relying on each other to move the chairs out of the way so they don't crash into them. The dance is partially about who has power, who must trust in that power. The bodies magnetize to each other and the stage sets. Watching people put their trust in each other is movingly human—from the audience, we witness the vulnerability and the earned power of saving someone who has set off on a course from which she cannot save herself. We learn the steps before we know what they're saying because we trust the art as much as we trust each other. In 2002, Bausch talked with *The Guardian* about creating new work, "I feel my way and try not to be afraid. It is not just that the dancers don't know where we are going, it is that I don't know where we are going also. It is not just that they have to trust me, I have to trust myself too."

These are insights I would gain only after that fall that began the end of my dance career. After her retirement, Martha Graham's depression led her down a path of alcoholism and multiple suicide attempts. It was only by returning to dance in some capacity that helped her get back on her feet. At ninety-six she wrote her autobiography *Blood Memory* about her career in dance, and one of her final lines reads, "What is there for me but to go on?"

I wondered if and how I would be able to do something similar. The writing, the documenting of a life beyond dance felt like a way to go on. After all, I didn't have an injury that could prevent me from writing. But it turned out, learning to become a writer was only a step of many I would need to take in order to discover life beyond dance.

I had been a diarist all through my youth, though my entries were a text written by my body. The text was my body. When I began to write in earnest, it was to understand why I was having difficulty recognizing the world beyond the studio or stage. I felt removed from its concerns. But the deeper I dug, the more I saw a common condition. That dancers are performers and performers inhabit roles. I had been inhabiting the same role, and now I was being challenged to inhabit a different one.

Writing started as a way to trace my origin story in dance, to understand my exodus from the world of ballet, and the stripping of my identity. When I fell in the rehearsal studio that night, I didn't know I was going to be a writer. I had to relearn how to walk on the ground rather than fly in the air.

⚜

The music kept playing as I lay there. Its insistence felt unfair, like life continuing when I wished it would stop and wait for me to catch up. Peter and the choreographer and a few others who had been in the room were at my side quickly, but I don't know how they came so near me, or when. They must have run when they heard the collision between the floor and my small body, falling like a faraway star. Outside the sounds of night neutralized each other, canceling out the wind and fading voices and driving cars.

After I fell, a new story unwound like a spool of runaway thread. I lay on my back with my legs pulled to my chest, and people stood around me and spoke calmly, with wide eyes and forced confidence, the way they do when they try to pretend that everything is just fine. I looked up at the white ceiling and thought about my mother, who had been the first person to ever see me dance. I wouldn't see her until the next morning, when she and my father made the three-hour drive to pick me up from college and took me home to start the long process of healing from a fractured, ruptured spine. The night I fell, I lay on the floor in that ballet studio, my body lacquered with pain. My back was not the only thing that had splintered. I thought of how when my parents came to get me, they'd see how thin I'd become, and the secret would hang heavy between us. When they'd ask me where it hurt, I'd point to my back because I couldn't point my finger inside my own hungry heart and say, right here.

PART I

〜❖

1

Some people think of dancing as an expression of their power and passion, or as a hidden language only the body speaks. I envy those people for their effortless belief that dancing is more feeling than careful application of technique. All art demands our time and bodies, but unlike other art forms, like writing, dance allows someone to devote themselves to it as soon as she can walk. After all, most of us can pirouette long before we can read. In my family, we inherited our artistic vocations. When I was born, my mother took one look at my fingers curled around hers and declared I'd be a cellist. It's always felt like a parallel life, one I'm still devoted to in my imagination, but I've never picked up a cello. Her friend looked at the same folded fingers and corrected her: no, a ballet dancer, she said, seeing the natural placements of my hands as similar to the dainty way ballet dancers hold their fingers. My mother took another look and realized she was right.

My grandmother Kathleen, whom we all called Mita, had a false start to her own dance career; as a little girl she had taken free tap lessons at the local church so that she could be the next Shirley Temple. The plan was she'd save her Depression-poor family from their circumstances by tapping her way up a staircase, or on top of a piano or on board a ship. Mita's tap lessons were a desperate prayer, and in them bloomed the belief that dance could change the course of her life, but like so many dreams in those days, they weren't what pulled her family out of being broke. Time and the New Deal did that. When she was seventeen, Mita ran away from Texas to marry my Air Force pilot grandfather on the promise that she'd get to travel the world. By marrying someone with a promising future, Mita shrugged off the ordinary childhood that she'd spent killing rattlesnakes in the dusty yard of her family's San Antonio house— her sights set on high culture and social status.

While my grandfather was leading bombing missions over Germany, Mita moved back home, got braces, and went to two years of college in San Antonio. Once he was back, she was never fully convinced she wanted to be married to him, although they were married for sixty years, until she died—but all three of their children remember tension, hurt feelings, my grandfather's anger, his PTSD, and Mita's disappointment that she'd married someone who wasn't emotionally available. Still, she made the best of it. Early on, they got a tiny Christmas tree for her favorite holiday, and because they didn't have any ornaments, she decorated it with her clip-on earrings. Her children came to know and love the "Mita Christmas laugh," something I've tried for years to imitate but can't quite get right. It involves inhaling as you laugh, as though you're choking on joy. Despite her simmering disenchantment, Mita was always full of love and excitement and charm. She was our home, and she carried and planted our dreams for us.

In her early twenties, Mita had my aunt Michelle, whom we called Ñaña, and six years later, my mom. By then, my grandfather was a career colonel in the Air Force, and they moved to Ecuador for the first three years of my mom's life, where he was the Air Force attaché. My mom remembers very little from this time—a wall around their house that often got spray-painted with "Yankees Go Home" in Spanish; the altitude sickness she got that culminated with my grandfather flying her to a hospital at a lower altitude, where she exited the plane to the doctors waiting for her on the runway and announced, "Yo quiero una Coca Cola, Papa"; a song about a pancho verde she used to sing with her nursemaid. The rest were stories passed down to her.

My mom left Ecuador when she was three, and they all moved to Washington D.C., where my grandfather did something secret for the Pentagon.

"He practiced taking pictures of us with a lighter," my mom said, describing his James Bond-esque gadget. "Then he'd go to parties and take pictures of all the guests." But when I asked her what the pictures were for, she told me that information died when he died. "It's probably good we don't know," she said.

In Washington D.C., Mita had my uncle, five years younger than my mother, the adored only son of the family, whom Mita called "the young prince." A year later, they moved one more time, this time to Manila in the Philippines, which my grandparents, aunt, and mother always remembered as though it was bathed in a humid, dusky light. It was a golden era, a time of isolated wealth, hairdressers, and manicurists who came to the house to prepare Mita for cocktail parties. She had the life she had tap-danced for.

In Manila, Mita enrolled my mother and Ñaña in ballet classes, and took some herself. The sweltering work of dancing in Southeast Asia was broken by the cold fizz of a bottle of orange soda, fresh out of the vending machine in the dance studio, so icy Mita would shriek at them not to drink it so fast or they'd stop their hearts.

Mita saw ballet as something well-bred young girls did, and she wanted her own children to be well-bred in the manner that came with her own ideas of upward mobility and social status. She wanted to give her daughters the opportunities she'd never had as a child, and encourage their own grace and discipline.

Mita took my mom and aunt to see Beryl Grey, an English prima ballerina and eventual dance partner of Rudolf Nureyev, when the Royal Ballet came to Manila on tour. The program from that tour says the gala performances took place over three nights in May 1961 at the Rizal Theatre, although it doesn't say what they danced. Mita and my aunt took classes with the Royal Ballet during their visit, something Mita talked about for the rest of her life. When I asked my mother whether they did that because they were talented dancers, she told me no, it was because they were American. Their status as white Americans in this post-war era must have contributed to the family's sense that things were possible for them in the Philippines that would not have been possible in the United States. Money, race, and status bought them more there than it did at home.

Another thing it bought them was five full-time servants, something wholly unknown to them as middle-class Americans. Margarita did the laundry and gave my uncle butterfly kisses on his cheeks. Alfredo was the chauffeur, Nati was the nanny, and Rody was the houseboy, whom Mita would convince to shinny up the coconut tree in the yard to bring her a fresh one. Their cook, Toni, told my mother stories about how terrible the Japanese had been during the war, sometimes scaring her with the anger and hatred her memories brought up. My mom remembers palm trees everywhere and the heavy blanket of the air, and when they went into town, the call "Balut!" from the man selling the boiled duck embryos in the eggshell.

The family parties in the Philippines left a flash-exposed image burned in my aunt and mother's memories—of men like my grandfather in white mess jackets and the stylish women who wore pearls knotted down their backs. At Christmas, since there weren't Christmas trees in the country, the family got a bare tree and spray-painted it white, hanging pearly capiz shells from its branches. One year when Mita and my grandfather were hosting a Christmas party, one of the servants cut down and decorated a tree for her. "Build a raft for it," she requested, "so we can float it in the pool." They built the raft from bamboo and tethered it to the Olympic-sized pool so it wouldn't float around. Mita, Ñaña, and my mom poured wax over string to make candles in custard cups, lit them, and floated them around the Christmas tree, tiny sparkling lights like stars in the water. The guests were their friends and my grandfather's colleagues—the head of the Philippine Air Force, ambassadors from Australia, Canada, South Africa, dignitaries from Malaysia, Vietnam. Mita had a friend, the wife of the Korean ambassador, who wore a traditional hanbok dress my grandmother loved. Although she was a full foot shorter than Mita, she sidled over at a party and used her own body to secretly measure my grandmother's, pressing her arm discreetly against Mita's, her legs and the front of her body, so she could deliver the measurements to her seamstress who made Mita her own hanbok. At the Christmas party, my mother remembers piles and piles of shrimp and men in white who sliced roast beef. Near the twinkling pool, a four-piece band played music and people swayed in the humid night.

In the present day there are three major dance companies in the Philippines, all of which are relatively new, a colonization of other, smaller companies, but at the time, Mita, Ñaña, and my mom took classes at what is now Ballet Philippines. There, they learned ballet, and at school my aunt and mom learned Filipino dances—my mother learned the tinikling, a dance with two poles, and the itik-

itik, a folk dance, while Ñaña learned the pandanggo sa ilaw, in which the women balanced lit candles on their fingers and on top of their heads. These dances delighted Mita, who saw her daughters' worlds expanded and expressed through various dance styles, both Eastern and Western. Dance represented more to Mita than just a way to move her body, or a way for her daughters to learn good posture and graceful movement. It represented opportunity and femininity, and their access to expensive training gave them a chance to have an entire audience's worth of eyes on them. It was the opposite of Mita's Depression-era Texas childhood, the opposite of being trapped, or settling, or living anonymously. Ballet taught my grandmother how to be a woman, and she taught my mother and aunt those lessons in turn. Their yearning would be my inheritance.

In ballet they all learned to shape their muscles in studio mirrors, following rigorous training and the example of the older dancers. When Ñaña was a young teenager, she invited some of the dancers over to the family's house in Quezon City, an hour north of Manila. My uncle, who was about three, walked in and saw a handful of male dancers in their living rooms. "Are you ballet dancers?" he asked them. When they said yes, he famously replied, "Well I'll be goddamned."

When the company performed *Pictures at an Exhibition*, a ballet based on Mussorgsky's score, my mother danced the part of the little girl who wandered through the art gallery and watched the pictures come to life. She remembers a tall dancer named Mari Paz who had lots of personality onstage, a way of connecting to the audience and earning their love through her dancing. Mita and my aunt were in a televised version of *The Nutcracker* with the same company—Mita as a lady fanning herself at the party in the first act, and Ñaña as the Arabian dancer. My mother says none of them were very good, but all of them subscribed to the belief that dance was the shortcut to an idealized life.

But eventually, after my grandfather's job was up, they had to move again, so they set sail for the United States, arriving on my mother's birthday to the news that Marilyn Monroe had died. Life in upstate New York was different. Mita bought them coats that fall at the thrift store. She could make all of life into an adventure, but her imagination and resourcefulness were no match for this transition. My mother tried ballet for another few years, Mita driving her to the better, more expensive studio, farther from their home than the lesser studio nearby, but my mom realized as she crested adolescence that she preferred drama to dance, which asked different things of her. Ñaña must have realized she was never going to be a professional ballet dancer around then too, so she joined the cheerleading squad in her high school and enjoyed the popularity it ensured her. After college, she married someone from West Point no one in the family could stand, most of all her. She thought it was the right thing to do. Whereas my grandmother wished she'd had a better education, Ñaña wished she hadn't settled for security, but both felt they'd failed at living the lives they'd envisioned. In the Philippines they'd developed a taste for grandeur and refinement. Their real achievements—being kind, loving, funny, and the beating heart of their families—were visible to everyone but them.

Eventually the family moved to Santa Barbara, California, where my grandfather had grown up. My mother and uncle went to high school there. Ballet had become less of a focus for the family as my mother and her siblings got jobs and got married. But the family's ballet dreams were reignited with the birth of my cousin Paige, my aunt's daughter, who the family thought, perhaps, was born to dance. This is when the family developed the name "Mita," short for *mamita*, which Ñaña had engraved on a bracelet for her mother when she came to meet Paige.

Ñaña made sure Paige had a camel coat and leather boots, an expensive haircut and ballet lessons, even when she didn't have the money. Ñaña called her Scottie Fitzgerald after F. Scott and Zelda's daughter, as if she, too, were a "beautiful little fool." When she was eighteen months old, her father started a parade of men walking away from her. She had three fathers before the final one adopted her as a ten-year-old. Paige always had a gap-toothed charisma, even after the gap closed. (The hole that was opening inside her proved harder to fill.)

As soon as she was old enough, Paige began ballet lessons. There's a picture of her in ballet class at about six years old hanging in my parents' house. She has a "Hamill wedge" haircut after Dorothy Hamill, with chic bangs incongruous with her young age. She stands with her leg in tendu to the side, her arms in fifth position over her head, and she looks up at her hands, a tooth missing. What you can't see, unless you're looking for it, are the unrealized ambitions of her mother and grandmother she's carrying.

My mom grew up too. She went to college and majored in English, fell in love for the first time with a man she didn't marry, and then another one. After Ñaña left her second husband, my mom lived with her sister and Paige, sharing a bed with Ñaña while Paige slept on a pallet on the floor. Paige was desperate to please her mother. My mom remembers my aunt yelling at Paige not to drink milk when she was thirsty. "Milk is too fattening!" she yelled. "Milk is food! Drink water if you're thirsty!"

"Why is my mom so mad at me?" Paige asked my mother, who folded her into her own body so Paige could take refuge. She could not explain to a little girl that my aunt was mad at herself, and saw Paige as way to correct her own disappointments.

Ballet was that chance. When she was eight she was a soldier in *The Nutcracker,* and wore the same costume I would wear a decade and a half later. Even as a child, Paige spent a lot of time getting her body right in the mirror, pinching it in some places, sucking in her stomach and turning sideways, eager to please people, and aware of how to earn that pleasure. As she got older, she was the star of her ballet studio, and I imagine she felt that heady lightness of eyes in the dark theater, looking for her beauty and finding it. Ballet must have been both an escape from her need to feel worthy and proof of her worthiness.

My mom acted in local theater productions, got her teaching credential, and began singing in the choir at the Episcopal church where my grandfather had gone before the war. At some point, a woman she barely knew at the church—the one who eventually told her I'd be a dancer, not a cellist—asked her if she'd be willing to come to dinner to meet their recently divorced friend, who had two small daughters. "If anything had happened to my husband, I might have fallen for Michael instead," she told my mom. My mother, in her late twenties at the time, thought this sounded like a lot of pressure, but she agreed to be polite.

Michael called my mother before the dinner so it would be less awkward when they met (although making small talk with a stranger on the phone sounds much worse than making small talk in person). He was an English professor at UC Santa Barbara who specialized in Renaissance theater. They both loved *Emma* by Jane Austen and he offered to loan her novels by Barbara Pym. "He sounded like Gregory Peck in *To Kill a Mockingbird* on the phone," my mom told me. They talked for three hours, and decided they wanted to meet before the blind date dinner party, so they had dinner at a small French restaurant that no longer exists. By the time they showed up the that dinner party, they were already dating.

Maybe everyone thinks her parents' origin story is mythical, but in my own parents' I see the seeds of the life they aspired to, and seeds of myself. I see how my mother would have fallen in love with my father for his job, all the books in his life, his research abroad, the way he took care of my sisters and visited his family in Seattle every summer. My mother would have seen how well she could fit into all of this, and how it would define her life. Within six months of meeting, my parents were engaged. My father was Catholic and my mother converted for him, going through catechumen classes and a Rite of Election ceremony at the Mission, and she never looked back. Two months after they got engaged they were married, the day after Christmas, at the Episcopal church where my mother sang in the choir, by my father's Catholic priest. My two older sisters, from my father's first marriage, were her bridesmaids, along with my aunt and Paige. My mother wore a pale blue ribbon in her black hair, a nod to my father's latest academic subject, Edmund Spenser, whose ode to his own second wife, Elizabeth, on their wedding day included the line: "Bound true-love wise with a blue silk riband."

The two of them went to Italy or England for my dad's research in the summers, so my mom's career as an elementary school teacher dovetailed nicely, since both had summers free. My mother learned to cook, took care of her stepdaughters, read books, and went to operas with my father. Their life was cerebral, and one that cultivated an appreciation of fine arts, which dance counted among, even if it is always considered to be on the bottom of the heap.

Before I was born, my dad probably didn't know the first thing about ballet. He certainly learned about it as soon as I came along and my mother's family decided I was born to dance. When I was born, my mother dressed me in overalls and pants—whatever she thought was practical and she could save for a younger sibling eventually, but the people around me couldn't help but give me dresses to make me look like a tiny ballerina.

I spent my first summer in Rome while my father was researching art and iconoclasm at the Hertziana, an art history museum with a doorway that looks like a mouth. My mother was jealous he was in a cool, stone basement while she, my sisters, and I walked the dusty streets, stopping for water at the public spigots around the city and splashing it on our necks. Pictures of this time period take up a disproportionate amount of wall space in my parents' house. I see my mother at the same age I am now, her dark hair pulled back to reveal a face nearly identical to my own. I see myself as a baby sitting on her lap—between columns at a church, holding a bouquet of pink roses given to me by a woman decorating for a wedding, on St. Francis of Assisi's altar where he blessed the animals, breastfeeding gustily, getting a bath in the sink from my older sister.

As soon as I was walking I was dancing, which is probably true for most people who use their bodies as their primary modes of expression. One of my very earliest dance memories was of going to see Paige dance the role of Coppélia, the spotlight chasing her across the stage as she danced in pointe shoes, suspended weightless in my memory. It was thrilling to watch her transform into a ballerina and then back again to my cousin afterwards, someone who loved Diet Coke and Snoopy, who imitated characters from movies and played pranks on my aunt. Even offstage, I recognized the gifts dance bestowed on her, the slip of her body and her awareness of our eyes as we watched her cross a room. Because I loved Paige, the easiest way to become her was always to enroll in ballet classes as soon as I was old enough—ballet seemed like the genesis of her loveliness. To the women of my family, the role of the ballerina was our vision of the kinds of women we could be— the effortlessness and camaraderie of a rehearsal studio, and the hair spray and tulle of a performance.

Mita gave me a VHS tape of Mikhail Baryshnikov's *The Nutcracker* as soon as I could walk, scrawling my name, Ellen Kathleen (named after her), in huge red letters across the top as though it was another title. That video became a religion to me, something I believed in that was greater than myself, that transcended family, future, or my body's capabilities. It built for me a world that made sense.

The Nutcracker is based on an E.T.A. Hoffmann fairy tale from 1816, in which a young girl, called Clara Silberhaus, cuts her arm badly during the battle between a seven-headed mouse king and her nutcracker doll, and hears terrible stories about a mouse mother who avenges the deaths of her children. The mouse king brainwashes her in her sleep, and when she wakes up, she marries the nutcracker prince. The version most of us know was rewritten for a younger audience by Alexandre Dumas, who changed Clara's name to Marie. Both names are used interchangeably in ballet productions.

Clara has been as aspirational role for young girls since the ballet premiered at the Mariinsky Theatre in St. Petersburg in 1892 to sold-out audiences. It's hard to imagine hearing Tchaikovsky's overplayed music for the first time, and the original reviewers were underwhelmed, calling some of the choreography "confusing," the libretto "lopsided," and the dancing "the most tedious thing I have ever seen."

After the Mariinsky Theatre stopped performing the ballet and its dancers were forced to flee across Europe, the ballet showed up in other countries before it made its way to America during World War II. But a decade later, when George Balanchine staged the ballet for New York City Ballet, he resurrected the version he'd learned as a young boy in Russia, modernizing it for a new century of balletomanes.

Clara is often young girls' first introduction to ballet. The ballet is performed by ballet schools all over the world. If someone sees only one ballet their whole life, it is often *The Nutcracker*. There is a role for everyone, and casting it every can be a way to measure a dancer's progress as she cycles through roles to become a soloist.

On my beloved VHS, Baryshnikov was the prince and Gelsey Kirkland was Clara: her face was so familiar I looked at it and saw my own. To say I watched it every day sounds like an exaggeration, but it's not. I don't remember ever being bored as a young child because I was too busy practicing my arabesques in front of our small television while my older half sisters did their homework and my parents wrote and cooked and did whatever adults do. But I had ballet, and the characters of that world, to guide me through those long afternoons. Their dramas were my dramas, their lessons my own.

By the time I was two, everyone talked about how I'd start lessons as soon as I could enroll. My mother used it as leverage to get me to do things like eat my vegetables—"Ballerinas eat their vegetables," she told me often when I was young. Paige watched *The Nutcracker* with me in our living room and because she was a dancer, she could watch the choreography and then teach it to me. "Give me a pas de chat, pas de chat, coupé, pas de bourrée," she told me. And even before I knew written language, I could transpose this verbal command to my body, give the words meaning and life without yet knowing they were French words with specific meanings. The language meant something when I used my body to respond. Paige taught me to speak that way, and she was the only person I thought could really understand me, and reply.

Although all the women in my family—my grandmother, aunt, and especially my mother—were my fierce and constant supporters, Paige was my most encouraging dance teacher. She taught me never to lift my foot off the floor without pointing it, how to turn out from my hips rather than my knees. She told me to tuck my thumb into my palm for ballet hands, not to let it stick out stiffly. What Paige could never tell me, because she was just a teenager herself, was how consuming a life of ballet could be, and how devastating it would be to lose it all.

⁘

Mita, my mother, and my aunt took Paige and me to *The Nutcracker* later that year, when I was so young I can only piece the memories together from pictures and stories. I wore white tights and Paige put my hair in a bun like a baby ballerina, like hers was when we watched her in *Coppélia*. Watching *The Nutcracker* live, onstage with the symphony and the boys' choir and the dark rows punctuated by exit signs, I learned that ballet was up to interpretation. While the video I was used to watching at home had four men as harlequins, the version I watched onstage had Mother Ginger, a man dressed as a woman with small girls in bloomers—her gingersnaps—under her skirt. They were the youngest dancers onstage, about seven years old, and I could envision starting with these roles, danced by little girls, and all the long time and hard work it would take to be a real ballerina like Paige.

But by this time, Paige was a senior in high school, and my aunt realized that Paige was now facing the same crossroads she had once faced about ballet—namely that if you weren't going to be professional, was it worth facing the disappointment and rejection of trying and failing to make it in a company? Out of a desire to protect Paige from these feelings of failure, she convinced her to stop dancing and become a cheerleader, as she had. The transition from ballet to cheerleading had been a turning point in my aunt's life, when she'd gone from a shy little girl to a confident teenager, and she envisioned the same for Paige. Almost overnight, Paige was surrounded by friends and boys at high school. When she got mono, the living room filled with get well cards and bouquets from boys who missed her. Still, her younger brother, my cousin Matt, remembers her crying for the rest of her life when she watched ballet.

"The only time she seemed like she was alive was when she was in the dance studio," he told me. "She smiled the whole time."

For me, though, life as a dancer was just beginning. I asked my family to call me Clara because watching Gelsey Kirkland in *The Nutcracker* was no longer enough—I wanted to become her. I still watched that beat-up VHS tape nearly every day, wearing different dresses or nightgowns to match Kirkland, practicing her same wide-eyed reaction when she realized she'd left her regular life and entered into a dreamworld with her nutcracker prince. During her fantasy, the face of her godfather, Herr Drosselmeyer, is superimposed over the stage as she dances. She reacts to his gaze, bourréeing away from him into the waiting arms of Baryshnikov, her prince. To be a dancer, it seemed to me, was to be watched, to dance because others willed it.

I loved Baryshnikov because Paige loved him, and that was enough. We called him "Misha" because Gelsey Kirkland called him that in her memoir. He felt like a close friend of ours. When a ballet friend took me to see him perform for her birthday one year, I ran home as soon as the film in my disposable camera was developed to show Paige the pictures, his autograph in my program. "Someday you'll have a dance partner like that," she promised me, and I believed her.

We especially loved him in the movie *White Nights*. Baryshnikov plays Nikolai "Kolya" Rodchenko, a ballet dancer who defected from the Soviet Union, just as Baryshnikov did. Rodchenko's plane to his next performance crash-lands in Siberia, where he links up with an American tap dancer played by Gregory Hines. Paige loved the scene in which Baryshnikov tap-dances with Gregory Hines; we watched it over and over, trying to learn the dance vocabulary of tap, unfamiliar to us both. But her favorite part of *White Nights* was the scene in which Hines challenges Baryshnikov to do a pirouette for each ruble in his pocket. He has eleven.

"Eleven rubles?" Baryshnikov says, weighing out whether this is possible. "Okay." He takes off his jacket, walks to the center of the studio floor, and in his leather-bottomed street shoes, flawlessly executes eleven pirouettes. "Eleven pirouettes, eleven rubles," Paige said to me often, which came to be a dare to try something new, something that seemed impossible, but that the body could do even when the mind could not believe it.

Each Christmas I got ballet slippers, which I was not allowed to wear outside because real ballet dancers didn't do this. My father would dance with me woodenly around our dining table, but even

then I knew he was only doing it to humor me. "Carry me the way
the handsome prince carries the princess," I said, meaning my
body draped across both his arms, my head against his chest. I had
a vocabulary for helplessness, for dependence on a man saving me,
before I could write. But because my father had no inclination to
dance, I began praying out loud, every night, for a younger brother
"to be my dance partner." When my mom told me she was pregnant, my parents warned me it might be a baby sister, since my
dad had two older daughters—my older sisters—and me. "I didn't
think it was possible for your father to have sons," my mother has
said of their belief that I'd have a younger sister before too long.
But when Brendan was born, I wondered if he, too, was born to be
a dancer—if, just as Paige and I had inherited Mita's love of dance,
Brendan had inherited mine.

My father saw music in much the same way Mita saw dance—
an opportunity his family couldn't afford when he was a child, so he
learned piano as an adult, and made sure all four of his children did
too. Every night he put on classical music while we had dinner, and
played it in the car, quizzing us on the composer and time period
of whatever was playing on the radio. My older sisters played piano
and flute duets, their bodies swaying in time to the music they produced, while I sat watching on the wooden stairs near the concert
Steinway left to them by their maternal grandfather. The piano was
a behemoth with ivory keys I learned to clean with milk and a rag.
But rather than move my body to the music I made like my sisters,
I wanted to move my body because someone else was making the
music and my body could not help but react. My family always had
dreams for where dance and music could bring us, the doors we
could pass through with these gifts, and how they could provide
shape to those dreams.

Dancer and choreographer Merce Cunningham once said the only thing that connects dance and music is that they take place in time. "If you put them together, they can take place in the same time," he said in an interview with *Fresh Air* in 1985. This is how my earliest dance happened—in time, long before memory captured it, existing at the same time as the music in my family's yellow Craftsman in Santa Barbara. There must have been music as often as there was dancing. "But the music, the sound, cuts the time up differently from the way the dance does," Cunningham said. "The music cuts it for the ear, and the dance cuts it for the eye." The spark lit between dance and music became my own tiny pilot light, a tight fist of love in my stomach. Before all the other things dancing brought to me—the control and sprains, the hunger and feeling of flight, it brought me that small flame that ignited the person I believed I was born to be.

2

Ballet and language are always linked for me. The language I learned to dance was gestural, a series of dots and dashes that added up to complete thought, a phrase of music like a sentence unit. I also started dance lessons at the same time I went through a linguistic shift—not major, a slight change in accent, vocabulary, but enough to rearrange me. Children are able to learn second languages with native accents until they are about seven or eight years old, and learning to dance as a child is like learning a language spoken by your body. As we get older, learning a second language becomes trickier, more slippery and elusive. The accent, for example, or the subject-verb agreement, might sound forced, studied. We make mistakes in second languages we learn as adults we wouldn't make in our native tongue. In my own experience, fluency is also easier for children in dance. The way we learn to move is nearly impossible to unlearn, and picking up another style of movement as an adult feels like pure memorization, a conscious forgetting of what comes naturally. Still, many of us try to patch together what we were denied as children—languages we wish we'd learned, dance classes we wished our families had sent us to. Just as expressions exist in one language that don't exist in another—the French phrase "seigneur-terraces" for people in coffee shops who stay for hours while only spending a few dollars, or the Italian "sprezzatura" for the nonchalance that makes everything appear without effort or thought—there are words I cannot translate from ballet to language. I can tell you what the French phrase "pencher" means, but it's impossible to describe the way the legs scissor while the arms reach in this step, or the both static and pulling quality to the movement.

Choreographer Pina Bausch saw the failure of complete expression of both language and dance. "There are situations of course that leave you utterly speechless," she said. "All you can do is hint at things. Words, too, can't do more than just evoke things. That's where dance comes in again." When dance fails, we have words. When words fail, we have our bodies.

⚜

For a fleeting and memorable two years, my family moved from coastal California to London after my father accepted an appointment directing the University of California study abroad program in the U.K. and Ireland. We arrived in London as soon as I was finished with kindergarten. Brendan, my younger brother, was walking but hadn't started talking yet.

Everything in London felt like a slightly off-kilter version of reality—richer-hued, more memorable than the familiar routines and landscape of home. I remember it so much more than most of my childhood precisely because it was different, a deep breath between the muscle memory of daily living. When I try to picture our family during that time, it seems strange we uprooted our lives from California's central coast, leaving behind the backyard citrus and the medicinal scent of eucalyptus for rural England's old vistas, and London's gray labyrinths, always in a simultaneous state of both self-editing and self-preserving.

My dad and I took the London Underground together. My grandfather had told me before we left that at each station a voice came on the loudspeaker telling us to "Mind the Gap." It became a white noise, an unconscious refrain by the time we got from Heathrow to the hotel.

We settled in leafy and storied Highgate, an 18th-century village in North London with a cemetery full of famous figures like George Eliot and Karl Marx. We lived on the Great North Road in a brick home—notable to me because I had never seen a brick building in earthquake-prone California. Everyone who came to visit said the home was small, but I was small too. It seemed big enough for the four of us, plus my sisters when they came to visit. We passed our days in the glass conservatory off the kitchen, where we ate dinner. That first summer I read my first chapter books by Roald Dahl and Enid Blyton, and Brendan stepped on a bee. We could pass easily through to the garden, where we helped my mother hang laundry to dry. My father began working longer days than he had in Santa Barbara, and we saw him almost exclusively on weekends, but sometimes I'd stay up late so he could read me *Swallows and Amazons* and *Treasure Island* when he got home, books about adventure and the sea.

Our first summer, before I began school, we went to North Yorkshire to see a ruined abbey. My mother said it was the happiest moment of her life. It was light until nearly nine at night, and the crumbling walls of the abbey were covered in roses. My parents went to a play and left us with the daughter of the B&B owner who fed us buttery noodles she called "pah-sta," the first "a" pronounced like the "a" in "apple." When my parents got home I told them about this exotic British dish, and told them it was like what we called "pasta" at home, but distinctly different because it had a different name. Language wasn't failing me—I could make myself understood, and understand others, even with their thick Northern English accents. But words seemed to shape-shift, taking up residence in the part of my young brain dedicated to new information.

My parents had promised once we arrived and began our new lives, I could finally enroll in ballet lessons. There's a picture of me under a tree in our front yard just before my first class, wearing a light pink wrap sweater and ballet skirt over my leotard and tights. My mother had taken me to High Barnet to buy my uniform, plus leather full-soled slippers and pink tights with seams up the legs. In the photograph, the ground is smeared with flower petals and I stand with my leg in a tendu, just as Paige had taught me, my arms in first position. I look calm and serious in the picture, perhaps feeling that although I had a strange accent and sometimes called things by the wrong names in my new life, ballet class provided an inevitable and familiar home.

My twice-weekly classes were taught by a South African woman named Mrs. Ford at a nearby dance studio on the high street. My mother signed me up for the British ballet technique, the Royal Academy of Dance (RAD), one of six techniques and the one, like my American accent, that would become my first dance language. The RAD method of ballet is rigorously classical, the style popularized in Russia in the second half of the nineteenth century, associated with the story ballets choreographed by Marius Petipa like *Swan Lake* and *The Sleeping Beauty*. Royal Academy itself was relatively new at the time, an amalgamation of other European styles adapted by English dancers in the 1920s. I took examinations based on the RAD primary curriculum beginning that year, and continued them through high school. RAD had a series of rules and exercises to memorize, and we students began right away to prepare for a life of serious dance scholarship that made our body into a study, a lab, a glossary. We became familiar with the architecture of the class, beginning with the barre exercises before moving into the center of the room to dance on our own. The progression from plié to tendu, degagé, frappé, the directions of our legs deviant, à la seconde, in arabesque, became as automatic as the letters of the alphabet. Like letters, they built into words and phrases too.

During our first class we learned the positions, but I already knew those. Most of what I remember about that first year of ballet is learning a dance that used a scarf. At the time I took the story the scarf and I were telling seriously—there was a narrative in my head telling me what motivated each movement, why I skipped forward in some parts and bourréed sideways in others. One part of class that is particular to the RAD grade examinations is that we devoted the last ten or fifteen minutes of each class to character work, which is based on European folk dancing, particularly from Poland and Hungary. For this portion of class, we exchanged our short chiffon wrap skirts for ankle-length black skirts with four colorful ribbons sewn across the bottom. We ditched our pink leather ballet shoes for black canvas character shoes with a short heel and an elastic strap to keep them on. In this outfit, we performed short choreographed exercises to classical folk music, gathering our skirts to point and flex our feet in time to the CD player, turn in, turn out, clap clap, feet together. I still remember this vocabulary too, although I have not done it since grade school, just as my mom can still perform the Filipino dances she remembers from her own childhood.

But ballet was still the center of each class in the RAD curriculum, and the reason all of us were there. It was the highlight of each

week for me, and something I often wrote about in my school jour-
nals once I began first grade, which was called Year Two in England.
Ballet and my American accent set me apart. The accent softened
and eventually faded, but my devotion to my weekly ballet classes
felt as much a part of me as my arms or legs.

The decorum of a ballet class dates back to the courts of the
Renaissance. We turned out our legs as Louis XIV, who is credited
with popularizing the art, did in his fencing lessons. We ended each
class with reverence, bowing or curtsying for the teacher. Proper
etiquette was imperative. Our hair was pulled up neatly into a bun,
our uniforms spotless, our chatter quieted so we could follow the
teacher's directions without asking questions except for clarifica-
tion of combinations. Ballet's aristocratic genesis is one of its most
lasting legacies. The position of a ballet dancers' feet, or turnout,
was codified into five positions by Pierre Beauchamps. "Turnout"
refers to the way the foot and knees are turned away from the body,
and became a hallmark of classical ballet, one I discovered early on
I was quite good at.

Although we lived in London, my dad's job meant he had to
travel to the campuses all over the British Isles to meet with students and faculty—this took us to Ireland and Scotland four times
in two years, and all over England (and occasionally to Wales) to
visit universities in cities and towns with old stone streets and
green, green sheep-dotted hills. We spent a lot of time in churches
too, where my dad was still researching iconoclasm, asking my
mom, Brendan, and me to find statues with their heads cut off so
he could photograph them. Brendan and I got very good at knowing which decapitated saint was which based on what each one was
holding—St. Peter's keys, St. Laurence's grill, St. Lucy's eyes on a
golden plate. Once a week or so, my dad spent a day in the archives

of the British Library (when it was still in Bloomsbury), where we'd meet him for lunch and then visit the dead mummy with red hair in the British Museum nearby. Brendan and I loved the ancient Egyptians and I learned as many hieroglyphics as I could.

My mother didn't work while we lived in London and says now it was a lonely time for her. Instead, she learned to cook Indian food, wrote a novel she put in a drawer, became friends with the other mums at my school, one of whom she still has a standing phone date with every Friday morning. Brendan learned to talk when we lived there, his accent completely different from the rest of our family's. "I'm the king of the castle and you're the dirty rascal," he would shout at us, sounding like a North Londoner. That fall, when we raked leaves for the first time in my life—southern California didn't have many deciduous trees—into a giant pile in the front yard, I threw myself into the pile while he scrambled to the top to shout that rhyme. He wore shoes like Christopher Robin— little navy T-straps—and floppy hair and cardigans. While the rest of us were still trying to become British, Brendan was fully fluent.

My parents noticed I spoke with an American accent with them, and sounded English with my friends at Highgate Primary School. School in London was, like everything, both wholly familiar and unfamiliar at the same time. We walked there every morning and walked home every afternoon. Both years, I had male teachers, one of whom played guitar and taught us songs I brought home for the whole family. "Cauliflowers fluffy, and cabbages green, strawberries sweeter than any I've seen!" I sang in an English accent, because that's how I'd learned it. My best friend, Nadia, was good at writing and never asked me how to say things like "garbage can" or "car" in my American accent as other students did, just to laugh at my strange way of talking. Her mother wore a headscarf and Nadia went to the mosque on the weekends with her family. We didn't see each other much on the weekends—in fact I don't remember ever going over to her house, and she only came to my birthday party one year—but we sat next to each other every day on the floor, spent all our "break time" together, and sometimes I tried to teach her ballet steps because she wanted to learn to dance too.

There was also Georges, whose French mother became my own mother's closest friend; Tom, who also already knew how to read; and Holly, whose father was the groundskeeper at an estate, and who was vegetarian and Buddhist. For PE a few times a week, which we called "games," we all stripped down to our underwear and undershirts and wore traditional plimsoll shoes to run around with hoops or balls or try to catch each other. The first time my mother came to pick me up from games and saw me in my underwear with my whole class, she said she was shocked. She thought it was creepy, she says now. "But when in Rome . . ." she told herself. She never said a word to me at the time, and I didn't know to be ashamed of my body yet, or to hide it for the sake of privacy, modesty, or physical boundaries. Instead, she granted me the gift of living fully in its capacity for fun and innocence as long as I could.

I kept going to ballet classes, storing exercises in my muscles to show to Mita and Ñaña and Paige when we got home. My mother took me to the Royal Ballet to see *The Tales of Beatrix Potter* during our second year in London, and I raced home to call Mita to tell her about Mrs. Tiggy-Winkle and Jemima Puddle-Duck, and hear her laugh in excitement. "Tell Paige I saw the Royal Ballet!" I demanded. "Tell her they wore pointe shoes like she does!" And she said she would.

Christmas in London was the most memorable season when I was small. Both my sisters came to stay with us—Meg was studying at Oxford during our second year there, in fact, so it was just a train ride to see her or for her to visit us. But my oldest sister, Kate, came too, and promised me when she got there she would take me to ballet class, and sit in the front and watch the new dance I'd been preparing. I was so excited to finally get to show someone new what I'd been working on that the day at school seemed to drag. When she finally came to pick me up to take me to ballet, I had been going over the new dance all day in my head. I had danced my own way across my brain while Nadia and I were asked to recite our times tables. I danced across my brain during break time, during art and music, during our school assembly. Once school was out, Kate brought my dance bag and walked me to my class, where I changed into my ballet uniform. I introduced her to Mrs. Ford, and found her a chair to sit on. As I did each plié, tendu, and ronde de jambe, I felt pride in my hard work, knowing I was doing something Kate would be proud of, that she had never learned even though she was already in college.

When the time came to move to the center of the room for the second half of class to perform our exam dance, my mind was buzzing. Mrs. Ford let me dance in front so Kate could see me properly. As I was dancing, I came to a part and stood still. I had no idea what I was supposed to do now that I had an audience. Mrs. Ford blew at me, because the wind was supposed to blow me backwards. But I misunderstood her cue, and instead blew back at her. She, Kate, and the other girls in the class laughed, and I felt my cheeks redden. They were not being unkind, but I had let myself down, and had my first ballet embarrassment because I had not yet learned to switch my brain off and rely solely on my body's memory of what came next.

In school we put on a Christmas pageant, and I desperately wanted to be the angel because the costume meant a silky white robe, paper wings, and ballet slippers, which I already had. Instead I was one of the wise men, and my mother had to make me a jeweled box for my myrrh. We processed in to our school auditorium to "We Three Kings," my parents and siblings in the audience, and I felt intoxicated by the idea of performing, of knowing lines or movements and having people watch how hard I'd worked to get it right. Christmas in London was cold, which somehow made it all feel more real. Those were the last two years I believed in Father Christmas too, that I believed he would find us although our vocabulary and traditions were not quite right.

A few days before Christmas Eve, my parents took Brendan and me to visit Father Christmas in Selfridges, a department store on Oxford Street, where we waited in an impossibly long line that seemed to coil and double back on itself through rooms and rooms, discarded mittens and tired elves surrounding us. When we finally made it to Father Christmas I asked for a stuffed panda bear and a new pair of ballet slippers, and Brendan asked for a red car he could pedal around in. My parents reminded us that English children left their stockings by the end of the bed rather than over the fireplace—which made sense because so many chimneys, including ours, were blocked off to control smog that threatened to take over the city in midcentury. That evening we went caroling in Pond Square with the rest of Highgate village. There was an alchemy to all of our voices the knowledge that we were all doing the same thing at the same time, for no other reason than to create beauty together. Now when I see things that remind me of those two years in London—a certain kind of chocolate sandwich biscuit we kept in a plaid biscuit tin, a pub's outdoor picnic table, a pair of Doc Martens—I feel that lift of my child heart I felt at Christmas, singing carols with strangers. I remember holding Kate's hand, Brendan's wind-whipped cheeks, the promise that in the morning, I'd have a new pair of leather ballet slippers.

This is where language fails: in communicating feeling adequately. To speak of the fever of finding my new stuffed panda *wearing* the ballet shoes that Christmas morning, or the mud-wet garden we dug away to plant once spring arrived, wearing our Wellington boots and Paddington coats, or the illustrations in the children's books my mother bought from church fêtes, a completely different canon from the children's books in America, with rhymes I can still recite. Only dance can give me those feelings without embarrassing me with their ardency. Now I can recreate the hitched breath of a pas de cheval, a step we did in the third exercise at the barre as we prepared for our Grade 1 exams. Language can be imprecise, tedious. Ballet is a connotative gesture, impossible to translate, but its syntax recaptures for me something of a very happy time. Ballet gave me a way to say, "I had to leave one life, learn how to live a new one, and then come back and forget and re-learn everything all over again."

Two years after we arrived, my dad's appointment as the director of the study abroad program ended, and we packed up to move home to California. Just before we left, Mrs. Ford, my dance teacher, sent my mother a letter about the importance of finding a school in California that taught RAD, so my ballet lexicon would not be lost. "I am really sorry you are leaving England but I expect you look forward to the return to the USA," she wrote in fountain-penned cursive. "I will miss Ellen. She is not only a physically lovely child. She is intelligent, serious, and talented and a real pleasure to have in class."

"It would be very nice for Ellen to return to America with a Royal Academy exam result to her advantage," she wrote, trying to convince her of the importance of my taking the exam for which I'd been preparing all year. "I would also hope, of course, that she could continue at a Royal Academy school. There are many in the USA (the Academy can give you details . . . on the best).

"I say this because the Academy syllabus/work is the finest and most detailed for young children and the Academy has a system to guarantee standards." She warned my mother to find me a *good* school, not one of those "cowboy schools" with no standards one can find "on every street corner" where I'd never meet my potential. In one of *those* schools, "We end with a situation whereby a) much talent is lost b) considerable harm to the child is done." Some schools, she wrote, put on "tacky shows" at the expense of proper technique, and she urged my mother to find me a school uninterested in putting on such displays. "Training a dancer is far more important than rouge and sequins," she ended the letter. My family, rigorously academic and involved in the opportunities afforded through application of study, memorization, and critical thought, took this advice seriously. When I was only six, seven, eight years old, I learned to approach ballet with the same reverence I saw my father apply to his love of classical music or Renaissance art.

I took the Grade 1 exam just before we left. My mother sprayed my hair into a stiff bun and drove me to another ballet school where an examiner from the Royal Academy sat up front and asked us to show what we'd been rehearsing all year. In RAD exams each group has four girls: the pink girl, blue girl, white girl, and yellow girl. We wore a small ribbon to show which color we were pinned to our light blue leotards, and I wore pink, which meant I was first at the barre, and closest to the examiner. I danced my very best version of the scarf dance, remembered all the exercises from barre to character to center perfectly, and learned that I danced best when I let my mind erase itself and trusted the memories stored in my muscles.

We had to have my results mailed to us back home in Santa Barbara, though, where my mother read them to me in the kitchen. "Posture & Technique: 17/20. Musicality & Dance Quality: 16/20. Line and Ease of Movement: 16/20. Rhythm & Style: 16/20. Detail & Sense of Performance: 16/20. Total: 81."

The examiner wrote at the bottom, "Well prepared and placed work, try not to lift shoulders at times. Very good study and dance." I passed "with distinction," the highest possible marks in the Royal Academy.

Ballet, like language, is a cultural code that becomes second nature. To this day, ballet technique affects the way I follow my own hand with my eyes when I reach for a glass of water, or hold my arms in front of me when I stand in front of a group of people. Every gesture means something, not just because it's familiar, but because it communicates what words cannot.

When Pina Bausch realized the difference in casting her eyes down or looking straight ahead, the small distinction created a noticeable difference in her choreography. "It's all a language you can learn to read," she said. The academic approach to dance I learned when I was so young gave me discipline and made me take ballet seriously, developing clear and attainable goals. Movement became a vocabulary I could forget about and return to, one that promised to bend me closer and closer to perfection in life, but most of all in dance. I saw no difference between the two.

3

We returned to Santa Barbara two summers after we left it.
My mother couldn't get over how much space there was between
houses. I couldn't get over the size of our backyard, which seemed
to have grown since I last saw it. The best part was seeing Mita
see us again; she laughed and clasped her hands against her chest
and took me swimming at the pool in her retirement home almost
every weekday during the summer. She sat in the shade in a wide-
brimmed hat while I did underwater flips under the afternoon sun,
a novelty after two years of unpredictable summer weather. She
cheered as though I were in the Olympics, told me I was strong
and graceful like a dancer. Sometimes she would let me take a nap
on her bed afterwards, playing with my hair until I fell asleep. Mita
supported me in everything I thought about, tried, or believed. I
told her everything, and her delight was my reward.

While we were abroad, once a week or so, we called Mita and
Granddad and told them what we were up to. I knew their number
by heart, even with the country and area code. "Mrs. Jones speaking," Mita answered every single time. Granddad's father was
British, so he was good at the accent, the idioms, the rhymes and
songs. But with them I could talk naturally, dropping any attempts
to soften my American accent, although after a while the new

vocabulary—"jumper" for sweater, "bin" for trash can, "boot" for trunk of the car—came naturally, and I forgot my old way of saying things. Besides, children living in different countries, learning different mannerisms and sensibilities, must have been natural to my grandparents, who moved around with their own children so many times. "Now I know how my mother felt when we moved to Ecuador and the Philippines," Mita once told my mother. "I took the children away from her, just like you have!"

Mita had promised me before we left that she'd come visit at the halfway mark between our two years there. As we drew closer to one year, she said they were busy, they couldn't make it, they had a lot going on. My mother told me years later she was as hurt and confused by this as I was, but it wasn't until we got home that we realized that while we were living in London, our family back home was splintering. My grandparents were hardly able to speak about what was happening in person, much less over the phone. While I was taking ballet lessons and learning recorder, Brendan was starting nursery school, and my mother was writing and taking us to playgrounds and museums, Paige was in crisis.

That first summer back, after we'd gotten my ballet exam results, my family drove a few hours away to a theater where a piece Paige had choreographed was being performed. Paige lived in the Central Valley, in the middle of the state, with Ñaña, her stepfather, and younger brother, where the hot dust clung to buildings and the water smelled like sulfur. My mother did her best to explain to me, as an eight-year-old, what was going on. "Paige has changed a lot since we moved to London," she told me before we saw her. "She'll be really different than how you remember her. She might look different and act different, but she's still Paige." She told me not to say anything if I was surprised, that we'd talk about it later. My mother was always good at explaining-without-explaining the horrors of life in a way that satisfied me when I was a child—the priest from our church who went to jail, the man who was killed in a park by our house, Paige's drug addiction.

Here's what we knew: Paige had gone to college, and then transferred to another one. Before we left she'd had a boyfriend, someone she loved terribly, who told her he was separated from his wife. As she'd fallen in love, Paige had begun taking modern dance lessons, and was finally able to return to the dance she'd missed for the last few years of her life. But then this boyfriend got his wife pregnant, and told Paige he could still date her too, but it would have to be a secret because he would soon have a baby. Paige felt responsible for her part in the betrayal, and considered this her second big heartbreak after the loss of ballet. She became unfamiliar to herself and to us in her grief, losing her sunniness, her sense of humor and fun. She stopped dance once again because it was too painful to face so much loss all at once.

Here's what we didn't know: Paige had had her wisdom teeth out while we were in England, and for the pain the doctor had prescribed her a course of Vicodin. But the combination of the heartbreak and the physical pain made her go through them too quickly, so she asked for more, and then more. She asked for so many the doctor cut her off, so she went to another doctor, and another. She called in prescriptions for herself when she couldn't get them legally anymore, and when she got to the pharmacy the police were waiting for her. So she spent the night in jail, sleeping in her own menstrual blood because she had been booked on the first night of her period, but even that wasn't enough to stop her dependency. Once my aunt and Mita bailed her out, she found new ways to get Vicodin. At one point, she told me years later, she was swallowing the equivalent of twenty or so a day. Her life, simultaneous to our own, had changed completely and irrevocably halfway around the world, and the rest of our family felt they couldn't say a word about it to us. I think now it was too painful to acknowledge, too broken already, beyond anyone's help or love or sense of possibility.

As we sat in the audience that summer, I marked the program with my finger to keep track of which piece was being performed, and how many more I'd sit through before I saw Paige's. I hoped after I'd watched it, she'd teach me the steps, and I could show her how much I'd learned while we were away. How much better I could now control each muscle. I wanted to be able to take her verbal cues and bring them to life, to show her how much closer I was to being a ballerina since I'd last seen her.

The dancers in Paige's piece wore knee-length blue dresses that caught the air around them while they turned and swiveled to swelling operatic music. But it wasn't Paige under the spotlight. It felt unfair that she'd done the hard work of looking at a blank stage and filling it with the ballet she pulled out of her head, but she couldn't dance it.

After the performance we waited near the artist entrance. I didn't recognize Paige until she got close enough to shout our names. Last time I saw her, she had been a thin ballerina, but her body was bloated and heavy now, its outlines more generous. Paige's transition from dancer to non-dancer was inseparable to me from her transition in how she looked. My child brain made up an equation to explain this: when she was thin, she was able to dance. Now that she wasn't, she couldn't. The rule, I assumed, applied to me too. She seemed out of breath, distracted, nervous. She laughed too long and too high at things that didn't seem funny, and shifted under our gazes. She was never still, always in motion. But with my mother's warning in my ear, I didn't say a word. Instead, I ran up to her and wrapped my arms around her waist. She smelled like cigarettes and hairspray and vanilla. Her voice when she said my name was high like a little girl asking for permission. She had the same game show smile as all the women in our family.

Our family has always celebrated each other lavishly. After Paige's performance, we went to Ñaña's house for dinner, all of us together again for the first time in years. My cousin Matt carried me around on his back and cracked jokes with Paige faster than I could laugh. I ate an Oreo, which I'd never had before, and eventually, Paige pushed aside the coffee table and taught me the first two measures of the piece we'd just watched.

◦✺◦

My parents loved high culture, but we always consumed it on a shoestring budget. When we went to the theater, we got rush tickets just before the shows started. My dad loved listening to classical music and opera, but he never bought a new car, his shirts had holes in the elbows, and his jeans came from Costco. He took us along with him on his summer research trips, but we stayed in the servants' quarters of crumbling old houses he paid for with research funds. My dad's best friend happened to be a Dickens scholar, also Catholic, who didn't have any children. My parents asked him and his wife to be my godparents when I was born, and they paid for so many of the opportunities I had as a child, including ballet lessons and a Catholic school education. My dad paid for the weekly piano lessons he insisted I begin as soon as we returned from London. He taught summer school for extra income to send my sisters to college and to send Brendan and me to piano. I knew there was no way I'd ever be allowed to quit, although I never loved piano lessons as much as I loved ballet. My siblings never wanted for anything, although we never had the right status symbols at school—the right backpack or notebooks, the right shoes or hobbies. As long as I had ballet lessons, I felt there was always a place I belonged, and always a place where I would be acceptable.

That first fall back I started third grade at San Roque, a parochial where I stayed until eighth grade. San Roque was strict—we had to stand up and greet our principal or the priest by name when they entered the classroom, and my uniform, a plaid jumper for the girls, had to be knee-length and worn over a white blouse with a Peter Pan collar. We went to mass at least once a week and prayed in the quad with the whole school each morning after recess. Once, a girl at my lunch table got sent to the principal's office for pretending her sandwich was the Eucharist—which we all did sometimes, but learned to hide after this. I learned to say the rosary during May, the month of Mary. My parents had given me a rosary for my first communion when we lived in London, and I worried its pink beads between my fingers as I learned to power down my mind in repeated prayer, just as I was able to do in ballet class. That first year back I felt strange, out of place again. I had the traces of a British accent, which I tried to hide. I used the wrong words for things sometimes, and felt I'd missed something important by coming late to a small school where everyone had known everyone else since kindergarten. I didn't like elementary school because it felt like I was always a step away from getting into trouble, that expression and independence were discouraged, and the other kids laughed at me for the way I talked. Ballet was the place I wanted to be. My ballet friends there were nice to me, and I was able to interpret and mirror the world I found there.

Following the advice of Mrs. Ford, my mother found me a local ballet studio where I could continue my RAD training. It was the same studio where Paige had danced, only there were new management and new teachers now. I enrolled as soon as I could, and began what they called Ballet 3, which had a similar uniform to what I'd worn in London. The best part was we met three days a week instead of just two. My mom had gone back to teaching fourth grade full time, so Mita took me to ballet classes near her house after school. Three days a week she and my granddad picked me up and took me to their house to eat a snack, do my homework, and get ready for ballet. Some days I forgot my ballet bag, so they'd have to drive ten minutes in the opposite direction so I could run in our house to get it. I always apologized, embarrassed to inconvenience her. "Just think of how many times you have remembered it," she told me. No one has ever been more patient with me than Mita.

At Mita and Granddad's house, Mita kept her cupboards and fridge stocked with my favorite foods. Sometimes, if I didn't have too much homework, she'd give me a manicure (no nail polish, which wasn't allowed at school), put egg white on my face for my complexion, and rub my feet. Mita was always touching the people she loved, rubbing our necks, holding our hands, stroking our hair absently. I rested my head in her lap while I read to her or watched a movie before ballet. She rented me dance movies she loved when she was young—we loved Shirley Temple's knees and Ginger Rogers's upper body fluidity, although Mita thought Fred Astaire looked "like a mosquito in tap shoes." Mita knew everything about my life in those days, sometimes even more than my mother, who was busy working and cooking dinner and trying to coordinate our rides to and from school. The days I didn't see

Mita I called her on the phone just to catch her up, and hear her delighted reactions. "You're the blackest little crow in the forest," she used to tell me. Her praise was extravagant, unearned, a hallmark of her love.

That was the December of my first performance of *The Nutcracker*, when I was finally the soldier. Paige and my mom glued our red felt cheeks on backstage before the performance. Mita brought me sandwiches during the three days I lived at the theater, and swore she could tell which of the twelve tiny soldiers I was from the audience, even though we all looked exactly the same.

Paige lived with us sometimes between rehabs or jobs, between hospitals or boyfriends, variously, fully. She was often around for months at a time before she'd disappear again, resurfacing in a hospital or psych ward or jail cell.

Here is a memory of Paige: I am about eight years old, and she sits on my parents' front porch, smoking a cigarette. She swings back and forth, slowly, on the wooden porch swing, and asks me to do a ballet combination.

"Pas de bourrée, pas de chat, step, step, chassé," she tells me. I do what she asks. I am wearing ballet clothes from my class earlier in the day, playing a soldier in *The Nutcracker*, just like she had sixteen years ago.

"Beautiful," she tells me. "Now let me see eight changements and four échappées." I do this too, bouncing up and down as though I'm spring-loaded, looking at her face the whole time, watching it for signs of pride. In memory, I have a pearly view of the afternoon, a Vermeer-like light falling across us as I danced and she watched. When people watched me dance, I took form.

"You can jump high!" she tells me. Her words are commands for my body, my body is a tool for her love. I knew one girl in my company held her neck too stiffly, so Paige worked with me to make sure I didn't. Another girl landed from her jumps too loudly, so Paige taught me to land toes first so no one could hear me.

Paige is great fun for the hours each week I see her. She can imitate anyone's mannerisms, voice, inflection. She does the voices of people on TV shows, politicians, our mothers. Mostly we talk about ballet, about the older dancers in my company I look up to, and she tells me their strengths and weaknesses, which I was too young to see.

It is on this occasion or maybe another just like it that I ask her a question that has been on my mind for a few days. "Paige, what is the difference between French kissing and sex?"

She tells me, and I stop dancing to listen to her.

"Have you ever done anything like that?" I ask.

"Yes," she said. She took a long drag, never breaking eye contact.

"Did you like it?" I asked, realizing how awful being an adult sounded.

"I liked it. You will too, someday."

"Have my parents done that?" I ask her.

She tells me more, and I know that even though I can already do the splits, there is still a lot of living my body will do.

❧

Paige chain-smokes and we play Clue as she detoxes the first, second, thirteenth time at our house. We play Clue so many times that I have a Clue-themed birthday party when I turn nine. I dress as Colonel Mustard, my favorite character for some reason, and when my friends and I are eating, we hear a scream, and run upstairs to find Paige, face-down in the kitchen floor, with a knife blade sticking up, and ketchup all over her back. She and my mother had set up a murder mystery, with Paige as the victim.

On the porch where she smokes and gives me instructions to dance, Paige lets me see the scars where she sliced her wrists, the skin pulled back together with black thread. She tells me she got them from falling. "I didn't want you to see this and be scared," she tells me. Years later, I looked for the scars each time I saw her, a railroad track of puckered skin, another story her body told. I realized then that she hadn't fallen at all, but that she loved me enough to tell me this lie.

Paige's body must have been a stranger to her, eventually. And it was a stranger to us too. We let that happen, and so did she.

I wondered, even back then, whether Paige was so interested in my ballet classes because she missed dancing herself. She could barely hold down a job for longer than a few months before she'd get fired without telling us why. Ñaña could grow angry with her, as could my mom and my uncle and dad. But Mita always gave Paige a bedroom and a place to come home to. I conflated Paige's loss of control with her loss of ballet. Her life became wreckage after she stopped dancing. I mistakenly saw ballet as the anchor of my life because Paige's fell apart without it.

❧

In her landmark introduction to feminist dance theory, dance scholar Christy Adair wrote that ballet has historically selected dancers "on the basis of a classical ideal of beauty, by reinforcing traditional sex roles and by the hierarchical structures of both the training institutions and the ballet companies." While male dancers have the freedom of their full movement, female dancers wear pointe shoes, an exciting but crippling rite of passage that places women on a physical pedestal while also hobbling them. Being physically hobbled would limit the ways I thought about myself, and how I understood my own agency in my life. But when I was twelve: how I wanted those pointe shoes.

My mother took me to the ballet store in town and had me fitted for my first pair. The woman who fit me talked about the importance of placing padding over my toes to prevent blisters until I'd built up enough calluses that I could figure out what worked best for my feet. I wore lambswool pads to start, although I switched to gel later once I realized how much they helped prevent my toenails from bruising.

The dance store had a back room full of pointe shoes, including cubbies with names on them for the special-ordered shoes of each dancer from the professional company in town and some of the older dancers at my own ballet school. I tried on several brands, standing at a short barre and rising to my toes so the shop owner could pinch the satin at my heel, help me test the shank and box of the shoe. I ended up with a pair of Freeds of London—I tried several pointe shoes over the years, but began and ended with the same brand. Freeds custom-made shoes for professional dancers. Some even had their own personal shoemakers at the Freeds factory. I dreamed that someday, I'd have this kind of relationship with my own shoemaker.

My first pointe class had chairs in the front of the studio for our parents. My parents were there, but so were Mita and my sixth-grade teacher Ms. Matthias, whom I loved because she was a ballet dancer and she exuberantly encouraged my writing. After we had danced for an hour or so, we all changed into our pointe shoes and went to the barre, where we did some relevés slowly, then quicker sous-sus to learn how to hop from plié to pointe. There's a picture of me at the barre between my two friends, reverent in the face of this milestone. My right foot is slightly sickled, meaning it was out of alignment in a way that could have weakened my ankle. But my teacher would have corrected that quickly.

Thus began my pointe shoe rituals. Every dancer has them, and they are as personalized and tailored to each unique ballerina's taste and feet. We began with slipping the satin shoes out of the bag, but from there, our customized liturgies began. It took hours to mash the box, bend the shank, scrape it down to prevent slippery bottoms, rip out the soles, sew the satin ribbons, burn the ends. We had to cycle through several pairs at once, using Instant Jet superglue to keep one pair hard for turning, save one soft pair for jumping, use a dirty pair for rehearsing and a clean pair for stage. I sewed on giant elastics to keep the shoes on my feet, taped my toes under them to support swollen toe joints. I was always asking my mom for a new pair, and she was always telling me she'd just bought me a pair, but once they were "dead," they became dangerous for the overstretched ligaments of my feet.

"It was a revelation," New York City Ballet dancer and Balanchine muse Suzanne Farrell said of dancing en pointe. "I loved it up there. I felt so important." I never felt like that about pointe; I was always distracted by the pain I felt. In fact, many of the injuries that chased me down years later began around the time I went en pointe. My dislike of pointe was never enough to turn me off of ballet, but I kept my shoes off as much as I could, which meant I was never completely comfortable up there. Around that time, one of our dance teachers told each of us in class whether strength or flexibility was our strength, and before she got to me, I knew what she'd say. "You're more flexible than you are strong, Ellen," she said. "You need to work on strengthening your foundation, not over-stretching your feet and legs at the expense of your lines." I should have listened to her advice, and I should have recognized the metaphorical properties of her diagnosis, but injury never occurred to me when I was young. How could it, until I experienced it?

⁂

The summer I was fifteen we went to Florence for my dad's research. Mita had been feeling sick, but the night before we left told us she was much better, and we should enjoy our trip. A flicker of worry crossed my body, but that, too, was easy to ignore or intellectualize. A week after we arrived, just after our jet lag had worn off, she called us and told us the doctor had just told her she had stage IV inoperable lung cancer. She'd been a smoker for years, but had quit before I was born. Her oncologist said she had anywhere from six months to a year, and she explained on the phone that she didn't want to do any chemotherapy in her remaining time. She was never any good at letting other people take care of her. She insisted we finish our trip, that she'd see us when we got home. I remember my mom crying in public often that summer, in the cool wooden pews of churches, over picnic lunches in parks and at home as we ate dinner. I think she wanted to be home with Mita but didn't want to disrupt our trip. Ñaña and my uncle were there with her, as was Paige. My sister Kate flew out to spend time with her too. I missed Mita so much it felt like a paperweight was pinning me in place at night.

Two weeks later, we got a call from my uncle in the middle of the night. Mita was in the hospital. If we wanted to say goodbye we needed to come home right now. We packed in the night as my dad called the airline. When we got to the Air Italia desk, the woman who checked us in told us a note popped up on her computer asking us to call my older sister, Kate, when we got there. We knew what that meant; I watched my mother's face grow wild with grief.

When she came over to us after hanging up the pay phone, she told us Mita had died last night. "She was struggling for air," she said, "So they told her we knew she loved us, and she could let go." A few minutes after that, she was gone.

She was the matriarch of our family, and all of us believed we were her favorite. She had planted my ballet dreams in me, and now she was gone before she could see them take root. My family huddled in the airport in Milan, a tight tangle of grief, and cried. The next day when my mom told Ñaña how our family had gathered and cried openly in public, she said, "The Italians probably just thought your oldest son wasn't coming home for dinner." We'd missed the goodbyes, the decisions about Mita's end of life, the countdown of her final breaths. I think she would have been glad we were spared that, but it made it all feel imagined. For years I had dreams she hadn't really died, that my family had lied to me about it because I'd loved her too much.

Once we got home, we walked around in a daze. I tried to become her in my grief—wearing her bright pink lipstick and gold bracelets, stealing her body wash from the shower and opening her closet to bury my face in her shirts. My sadness felt like I'd borrowed it from someone else. Some nights I lay in my bed and asked her to haunt me. I tried to feel her ghost around me, but I couldn't. She was already gone, and stayed gone. But still, I could conjure her in my mind so easily, the way she walked with slightly knocked knees, her voice, the feeling and smell of her hair. The way she loved me. It all seemed just on the other side of a veil I couldn't lift.

My mother cooked Mita's signature dishes for us every night—her curries and beans, her carrot cake and cornbread. In all the years that have passed since Mita died, I have never gotten over a desire to tell her how it all turned out. On her tombstone, she requested the words "Find the good and praise it." I took my grandfather there every week for years to bring her a bouquet of yellow roses.

⚜

Two months after Mita died, I was cast as Clara, the main character in *The Nutcracker*, which felt like Mita's final gift, prescribed in her handwriting on that old VHS tape.

"Where else is there to go when you realize your life's goal at fifteen?" my father wrote in our Christmas card.

In her 1986 memoir *Dancing on My Grave*, Gelsey Kirkland says of the televised version she danced with Baryshnikov, "Misha asked audiences to consider what happened to the child after the dream came to an end. What was going on in that little girl's brain?" Of the version she insisted on dancing, she wrote, "My Clara was still looking for the Prince in the last scene, even when the curtain came down. She may have lost him, but she would never lose her dreams, her ideals, most especially her ideal of love. She would grow into a woman of imagination. She would be wise enough to defend her place in the world."

Because that year was my seventh *Nutcracker* as a dancer, and I had watched Gelsey Kirkland dance the role of Clara with Mikhail Baryshnikov as her nutcracker prince, I had considered every surface of the part and her role in the ballet's story. Now, I have a complicated read on Clara—on the one hand, I remember spending the entire second half of the ballet sitting on a cake, not able to dance once I had my prince. But I also willed my nutcracker doll to life and set the ballet in motion, and it was *my* dream that afforded the audience two hours of holiday escapism. It was a princess fantasy in which I held all the spinning plates.

Rarely, if ever in ballet did I ever ask myself what I wanted, although I had a sense of what my version of Clara wanted. She wanted to be protected, but also to protect. She had one foot in childhood and one in the fantasy of falling in love. She let herself be surprised by her own agency, but she was an observer. Her best dancing happened when she thought no one was watching, although those were the times I felt the audience's eyes locked on me.

I was eager to know what was expected from me during *The Nutcracker* rehearsals, to learn the choreography precisely and then make it my own. I knew my strengths as a dancer, and how the audience would react to them. I knew I had a certain elegant, silken quality to my port de bras, that I could jump as high as boys, that my turnout was impressive. I knew when my teachers were going to compliment me before they said a word, and I knew how to show off when I needed to. And like all dancers, like all women, I was keenly aware of my own deficiencies, which I only thought of as such because someone must have told me, along the way, that my feet weren't ideal or that my leg should go higher in grand battement en avant. As an object, I knew my angles, and I knew how to hide the parts of myself that weren't as pleasing to the audience.

Ballet was choreographed, and it gave me the false impression my life could be choreographed as well. I was asking to be watched as Clara, but I also danced for the sheer joy of disciplining and strengthening my muscles, stretching them so that I had a greater range of movement. In ballet classes before our nightly rehearsals began, my teachers made me wait to jump with the boys because I could jump higher than any of them. When I jumped, I was aware that people couldn't believe how high I went—they laughed, pointed at me, their faces caught in the same amazement I had when I watched Clara in *The Nutcracker* as a child. But more than that, I was aware of my own weightlessness, and how good it felt to fly.

Still, as I witnessed my body's strengths in the mirror during that season, I found them beautiful. But the satisfaction came from watching myself do something well rather than the joy of movement itself. Only once in a while, at the end of class when we did grand allegro across the floor I'd catch some air, and without looking in the mirror, feel the sort of blankness of mind that felt like pure happiness.

After each performance as Clara, I felt my beautiful self take shape in the audience's eyes—they drank me in with their gaze, so I became liquid. I might have danced the role of a girl who created the imaginary world she wanted, but under the heady gaze of the captive audience, I would have done anything they wanted.

The local newspaper wrote an article about me the week before the performances, and in it I mentioned I was dedicating all my performances to Mita, who would have wanted to be there. We had a full symphony orchestra that adjusted the tempo of the music to my dancing—I could ask them to slow down certain parts if I wanted my adagio to be slower, more deliberate, or to show off how high I could jump, like a man. I loved to create a sculpture with my body that lasted for just a count or two. My whole family, from all over the country, came to watch. Under their gazes, the theater lights on my skin felt electric, transforming me into someone I felt was finally fulfilling my family's dreams, which I never thought to distinguish from my own.

By learning the choreography perfectly, I thought I was learning the choreography of my own life. I thought perfection was possible. I didn't stop to think about what came after Clara's dream was over, and where my own longing began.

4

I was fifteen when two Russian dancers—one from the Bolshoi and one from the Kirov—came to my ballet school to choreograph *Don Quixote*. With their Russian words and their overly turned-out feet, they'd dance the lead roles. Olga wore her flaxen hair pinned just above the nape of her neck in a golden fist. She seemed to be nothing but eyes and feet—the rest floating prettily in between in a cumulous arrangement. Sayat, with his hooked nose and smooth hands, spoke for both of them. At the end of a heavily accented anecdote, we students would look at each other's faces, searching for the meaning that would help us dance the way he wanted us to. I fell in love first with the roomful of dancers who wanted to please Sayat and Olga, and then with the two of them too.

Days began with a warm-up class, all of us bundled in rubber shorts and woolen socks, lifting our feet off the floor with the articulation of a tongue. There were laws that only existed in ballet. There were things our bodies knew without having to be told.

That the foot beveled to the side when pointed, the toes reaching for the floor. To relax our ankles into plié, to line our bent knees over our feet. To tuck ourselves into neat little packages and surprise each other with when we finally danced together in rehearsals.

I had learned from *The Nutcracker* and some of the other ballets

I'd performed with my school there were endless girls and only a few roles, only a few favorites, scholarships. I was hungry for each accolade, but knew how to perform the role of hard work, and how not to perform the role of neediness. They were different, and resulted in different prizes.

The first time I saw Olga dance it was through glass. She stirred the air she passed through, vague as a cloud. She was demonstrating something to a class before mine, showing them something she could not explain in English. With her back arched, the girls watching leaned into her, but she didn't seem to notice a thing.

"She's perfect," I said in the hallway, where I stood safely watching. I admired perfection, which seemed not only like an option in ballet, but like the only option. "Her back is more perfect than mine will ever be."

"Yours is so long," a girl named Caitlin said. She was ambitious without apologizing, which made her suspect to a roomful of girls. Caitlin was angling for a solo, one she had paid for private lessons to learn; she watched videos, got there early and stayed late, and still had a face full of raw neediness. Watching her dance embarrassed me, because I knew enough to contain the things she refused to hide. Although I needed as much, I needed most of all to look as though my success was accidental.

She worked too hard, accepted compliments, talked about a future dancing with schools or companies she should have known not to discuss out loud. There was nothing we could do for her at that point. She sat in the hallway before class and listed all the things she had eaten that day.

"Coffee, pomegranate seeds, popcorn," she said triumphantly. She drank gallons of water and then danced in rubber shorts to sweat it out, and when she danced all you saw were the bones between her breasts.

I was sitting back on my heels, toes bent under me, to stretch the tops of my arches. This was what I focused on every day. I thought that if I could have better ballet feet, I would be more like Olga. Caitlin saw me. "Do you want me to stretch your feet?" she asked.

She pushed the flats of her hands into my feet and the movement touched me with its insistence. It did not seem like it could change me, or threaten to hold me back. "Can you push a little harder?" I asked. I knew that a girl who pushed herself could push me too.

Caitlin stared at my locked knees in pink tights and counted down from ten. She would become other things as well, but she would always be that, a girl pushing hard on the feet of another girl, waiting for an audition to start. Other dancers milled around us like a snowstorm, and I looked at the pink bridge of Caitlin's nose as she forced my feet down. She was pushing so hard on my feet by then that she was starting to hurt me, so I watched her face for any movement in the corners of her mouth that might mean she was trying to.

When I had had enough, she traced my spine down from the nape of my neck with one clammy finger, and each bone she touched made me grow taller.

"Someday you'll grow hips and I will laugh," she said.

The teachers lined us up in a room with numbers on our chests and high-cut black leotards in a cattle call of hip bones. Sayat's movement was like a long yawn in front of us, steps rolling one after another. He showed us something and by summoning up everything we had ever learned, we could mirror it back to him as though we had just thought of it ourselves.

The only way to differentiate myself was to be superlative at something, and as we built our movements up through the audition, and people were called on, and the florescent lights flickered,

I knew my need for Sayat and Olga's love was greater than anyone else's, and that carried me through.

I danced right behind Caitlin during the audition, following the steps she did until I was surprised to look in the mirror and see my own face and not hers. She was no longer in my group. She had danced in the first group, and then danced with smaller movements in the back with each other group as well. Sometimes she went twice, which later we would call hogging the spotlight. Caitlin didn't care, though. She had her own set of rules and beliefs, and our whispers were too quiet to change her. Years later, I can see she was right all along.

There were cuts after the first hour, girls separated into groups, until the room shrank to a few girls dancing to themselves to prove they could dance for someone else.

After the audition was over, Sayat told us our roles, based on how we danced, but there were only a few solos and so many dancers.

"You are Cupid," Sayat told me. My role was to make Sayat and Olga fall in love as Basilio and Kitri.

"Who is Cupid?" I asked.

"Baby Ballerina, Cupid is the star of the dream scene," he said. "It's because of your arms and your size and your jump. But when you dance, you must look your mama papa," he told me, and pointed to the corner of the room, where the balcony would be if we were in a theater. It was a ballet studio in California, with wooden floors and a grand piano. But I understood what he meant, that I must dance for everyone I knew in the audience, for the last row of the balcony, who would also have paid money for their tickets. As Pina Bausch learned through her own trial and error, it meant something entirely different to look down as I danced—melancholy, coyness, introspection—than it did if I looked up and out.

Cupid moved like I did, like a quick argument that you look back on and laugh. During the following months of rehearsals, Olga walked apologetically around me as I danced, laying her cold hands on my shoulders to press them down and back. I took comfort in seeing myself in the mirror and knowing exactly what I was doing wrong, and what part of my body needed to be grabbed by someone else's hands and twisted and pulled.

In school during the day, I sat in my desk and ran through the dream scene in my head. In those bright white classrooms of high school, colorful bodies crossed back and forth, answering questions and worrying about grades. They mostly blur in my memory, just out of focus of what I was really thinking about that whole time. In sharper focus I see Olga doing the steps, and Caitlin behind me like a shadow, in her own sinewy and earnest style, as if she were trying to get Sayat and Olga's attention over my shoulder. Sometimes I wished they'd look at her instead so I could relax, and sometimes I wished they would both fall in love with me rather than with each other.

Every afternoon, in the hour or so between school and rehearsal, I went home and stuck my feet under the couch to stretch them (to help Caitlin along), and every day in class and rehearsal, Sayat and Olga would compliment my dancing, saying "Yes" and "Good, Baby Ballerina!" as I jumped and unfolded and turned. My feet were weak and sore, but Caitlin always stretched them without my having to ask until my toes touched the ground, and I always let her. She did it until I could not stand the pain anymore, and I felt proud I had withstood so much already. That hunger for pain was a void whose bottom I could not see.

In rehearsals with Sayat or Olga, their Russian accents were now familiar. Behind Sayat, against the piano, Olga nodded at me.

"You have costume fitting after we rehearse," said Sayat. "Costumes from Bolshoi Ballet in Russia." He leaned toward me and pulled my sweater down over my narrow shoulders, and in his eyes I saw my beautiful shape begin to form. Olga looked at him without expression, without blinking, unaware or unconcerned that she was being watched by all of us. I wondered if that's how two people look at each other when they are alone.

The very small costume I was to wear as Cupid smelled like cigarette smoke and had small gauzy wings. Upstairs, above the studio, the seamstress and Olga pulled the fabric away from my skin.

"Is too big here," Olga said, "And not big enough here." I stood on a stool and turned around and around and then when I stepped down they looked at my measurements with genuine concern. The costume mistress pinned me in, and I told myself that although the pins made the costume feel tight, by the performance I'd make sure it was loose again by losing some weight. I wanted to be able to take a full breath, and to see folds of fabric over my sternum when I exhaled. My costume, I realized, must fit for the ballet to go on. Without my costume, we could not have my scene, and without my scene, there would be no performance. Caitlin tried it on after, and showed me the places where it was too big for her even after it was pinned for me.

This is not a story where someone crashes or falls or is beat up. This is a story where Caitlin pushed her hands into my feet each day until one day she sat on them instead, and I didn't protest. After all, I wanted them to curve toward the floor like a body bends against the cold. When Caitlin sat, there was a gentle and slow crack. We were sitting in the hallway before a class in our rubber pants, and girls around us heard it too. They all lay on their backs with their legs in the air, or pushed against a wall, forcing their stretches a little more. There were bodies everywhere, and they all froze for the second when we heard a crack inside my foot, and then the second was a long time passing.

"Oops," Caitlin said, dramatically grimacing, her hands covering my feet. I was silent and focused inward, or downward, to the sharp and steady pain in my right foot, and began counting how many days were left until our performance to assure myself that I would recover in time to dance the role of Cupid. I had accepted violence from Caitlin, and inflicted it on myself.

"That's okay!" I told everyone. "It's my fault, I asked her to. It will be fine." I was cheerful, insistent, near tears.

People stood and the air moved wildly around us all. Someone handed me a bag of ice and wrapped it around my foot with a leg warmer. From inside the studio, the slow music of the grand allegro at the end of another class hung in the light. Caitlin was Cupid that night in our rehearsal, dancing my part as I watched from the floor, although she knew each step, I knew she was not as good as I was, and would never be allowed to dance that part. Bodies were the enemy, after all, whether they belonged to us or to the girls we danced alongside. We competed for Sayat's halting, accented praise, for Olga's eyes to trace us as we danced. We were two women competing for one role.

My foot didn't swell immediately, but by the time I unwrapped it in front of Olga after rehearsal, it was round and hot. Her eyes darted around, searching the room for a solution. I saw the wisps of hair at the nape of her neck when she turned her head from side to side, and in her face and her form was something I had not seen before. It looked like pride. I learned from her face the necessity of sacrificing the body to contort it into something perfect. The room was mostly dark, but for a few overhead lights buzzing, streaming over our heads and then down to the floor. She leaned over me in the semi-dark, and I knew she wanted me to give my life to ballet right then, as she had done, to be tougher than physical pain, to dance anyway. With my foot still in her lap, I lay down on the floor, submitting.

"I am here," my mother said, coming in the doorway, and like a miracle, she was. Someone had called her to come take me to the doctor.

If I had known, at age fifteen, the exquisite violence that would follow in the years to come, two ruptured discs and fractured spine, the dislocated collarbone, the eating disorder, the sprains and tears and rejection, I would still have stretched out there on the floor and surrendered to ballet, would still let Olga move my foot around in her hands and assess whether I had what it took to dance through injury while my mother worried in the door frame. I was always powerless before the stories I told, and the roles I danced, in order to earn love.

We went to an orthopedic surgeon soon after and on the white exam table, I made up my mind that I would not be absent from the theater in a few weeks. That season I had already sustained a sprained hip flexor and dislocated my pelvis. The doctor, predictably and perhaps wisely, told me not to dance, but if I had been the type to laugh in his face, I would have. I thought he was the one who didn't understand. Years later, I see that I am.

The story I told myself was that it was my fault I let Caitlin stretch my feet with her hands; my unclearness, my own ambition that broke my foot. It was my fault that I danced on it. I knew the stakes, saw them on the horizon, aimed my body high, and barreled over them.

My mother gritted her teeth and drove me to rehearsals and packed me dinners to eat late at night, in the studio, stealing bites between dances. She believed me when I told her my foot had healed and took me to the theater to perform. It was a world where people paid to see fleeting beauty onstage that I would dance a little differently each time. The dance left no trace behind, no artifact, only the moment of watching someone dance hundreds of feet away, and swaying in your own chair.

Nowadays, I don't feel any pain in that foot except a slight twinge when I walk too long, a talisman I carry in me of all the times I sacrificed my body because I thought it would make me a better dancer and a better woman. My feet weren't arched enough, and I stretched them until they broke.

Ballet excuses and glorifies a culture of dancing through pain, and that it relies on women's bodies to be the tools of its expression, forcing its rigid ideas of beauty even at the expense of safety and comfort. I learned through my injury that making art requires more of me than I was prepared to consent to.

⁂

Downstairs in the theater, below the dressing rooms, was a nurse—the mother of a former student whose number we had in case of emergencies. The ballet director had to call her to administer Novocain through a needle into my foot before I went on stage. I don't know what they told her—maybe just that we had to get through it, and maybe, she knew the face of a girl hungry for attention and gave me what I needed just the same.

She had a metal box she opened as I sat across from her, my foot in her lap, and measured the clear liquid into the needle. Caitlin came in to watch, and then stood backstage with me to make sure I went on and stayed onstage, ready to carry on should I buckle under my own weight, but I never called on her to do that.

And though I should have been angry, I couldn't blame her. She only carried through what all of us secretly felt: that other women existed to measure ourselves against, to hurt in invisible ways, to help along when we could. That other women were just another device we used to punish our bodies with our naked, raw desire.

My movements in onstage rehearsals were economical: abridged and inelegant. I was saving it all for the performances. Ballet wrote its own laws under the pretense of art. I'm impressed that after all of years of dancing on pointe, my feet have no chronic pain. The enlarged joints that came from dancing on point must have shrunk. I stopped before I ruined my toe bones, my ankles and knees.

My father said he winced in the audience every time I stood on my right foot, but here is the only thing I remember about being onstage: the spotlight draped across the stage like a hand. I danced to show how much I knew, and all the things I didn't know but wanted to learn. From the wings, Olga looked so near.

This is the way stories end when a body commits violence against itself. I do a final arabesque, and cannot come down. The audience is still clapping as I stand on my fractured right foot, and backstage I see people jumping up and down, beckoning me to come join them, pumping the air with their fists because they cannot believe I am still holding this arabesque on a fractured foot. It wasn't until years later that dancing on a numb and fractured foot seemed like anything other than survival.

5

The great paradox of ballet is its demand that dancers spend their entire career trying to make it look effortless. In reality, it requires control over every quivering muscle to elongate and support yourself enough to do even the most basic steps.

I spent the summer I was sixteen in Massachusetts learning this lesson for the first time, in a humid dorm with wooden ceilings and almost no ventilation at all. It was my first time away from home alone, and my first summer intensive ballet program. My parents let me go because I had gotten a scholarship. I loved the daily classes with the same girls, day in and day out. I found a home, striving alongside them. It was the only future I could imagine for myself.

I had driven to LA for auditions that year, lining up against the barre with girls from all over southern California, numbers pinned to our chests, hair slicked back, in a uniform row, trying not to blend only once we began dancing. Auditions were nervy and dehumanizing, mostly because I wasn't very good at them, wasn't very good at standing out in a roomful of girls, and I wished instead I could show the judges my beating heart, so full of ballet, or write an essay about how I loved ballet the most, even if I couldn't stand out among all the ambitious young girls alongside me.

Where a young dancer goes each summer says a lot about where she'll go once she finishes high school. Everyone heard the stories of the dancers who were plucked out of summer programs to go to professional schools, the ones that fed into companies. The stories we didn't hear were about the girls that weren't selected, but it never occurred to me that my life as a dancer would be anything other than exceptional. Once I got into a program and received a scholarship, I imagined how I'd come back to my regular ballet school knowing new combinations, having new friends and bigger dreams.

In Boston, I arrived at an old dorm full of young girls who immediately claimed me. Our first class felt more like sizing each other up than dancing with freedom and abandon, but as I looked around the room, I saw the faces of people who had come here for the same reasons I did—the love of ballet. That first morning, I met a girl named Grace in the hallway, who took me downstairs to her dorm room and introduced me to her roommate. I sat on the edge of her bed while they got ready for our morning class, pulling back their hair, making sure their dance bags had the right pointe shoes, filling their water bottles from the tap. I could have been watching myself in a mirror, each gesture was so familiar. That day and the weeks that followed, we fell into an easy rhythm together, attending ballet classes in a pack, eating our meals together afterwards, telling secrets, making wishes. This was the first time I'd felt this with a new group of girls, and it made me feel like acceptance, like it would always be available to me as long as I followed the unspoken rules.

The late-June Boston air made me dance like I had a blanket draped over me. Overhead, the ceiling fan spun dangerously on its axis, agitating the hot air, made hotter by our striving bodies.

Between combinations at barre, I stretched my feet with my hands, propped my leg on the barre, marking the teacher's choreography with my hands as she demonstrated it. Each combination felt like the start of a new day, full of possibility: that I would finally relax enough to show them how much I loved what I was doing. I pushed myself—my leg a little higher, my arabesque a little more staccato, my jump bouncier. By the end of class I would remember what had brought me here, that I was molding myself into my future self with each repetition and each tiny success. "Beautiful jump," our teacher said to me during petit allegro, and I knew I had finally shown what I could do if only given the chance.

Our roles were always waiting for us to step into, which made us compete to dive in first and fully. This was one of the reasons I loved ballet so much—there were always roles ready for me to play without having to look too deeply inside myself. What we personalized in our dancing during our first week—a gesture towards our male partner, the adagio that unwrapped us from a fixed point into languid lines from the tip of our pointe shoes to the air just beyond our fingers—were fragments borrowed from other dancers, pieced together into our own style in a carefully choreographed dance. We knew the right way to do every step, the right way to talk about our ballet idols—some of whom were there at the school teaching us. Desires that summer seemed simple: a "very good" from our ballet master, a triple pirouette on pointe, a solo in the summer program's final show, or at least a few steps in the front row of the corps de ballet. By the end of the first week, we discovered we all had a crush on the same teacher. One bright morning, when he walked over to me during barre and adjusted my leg, I shot my eyes across the room at Grace, who met my look with one of her own. We wanted nothing more that day.

During our second week, in the dining commons, we watched as Stephanie in Level D ate only fruit for breakfast, and pretended we thought it was anything but aspirational. After all, she was *really* good at ballet.

"I bet she has an eating disorder," Grace said, picking at her waffles, as though this explained her talent.

"She's really sweet once you get to know her," Julie said.

"Her legs are as big around as my arms," I said. Our friendship was largely predicated on our camaraderie against the forces that threatened us most as teenaged dancers: eating disorders, injuries, and not being good enough at ballet. I battled each of these threats with everything I had that summer.

That second week, I began battling another beast, something that began slowly and felt worse with each class. In the past few years, my back began to hurt when I did too much pointe work, but Mita used to take me to her chiropractor after school and he always seemed to piece me back together. Coming into the program, I had thought dancing more would make me stronger, less prone to hurting myself. But it did the opposite. That summer as I pushed myself to stand out, my back grew worse and worse each day. There was no chance for rest, and no chance to take it easy, cut a class or skip rehearsal.

The campus's medical center became my routine stop at the end of each day. There I let strong hands peel off my clothes and manipulate my legs, asking, does this hurt, how about this? The first time I went, they told me my pelvis had dislocated, and gave me a brace to wear under my leotard, something I was relieved I could hide from our teachers and my friends.

Each day, with my hair still in a tight bun, my face still red and wet from classes and rehearsals, I rolled the bottoms of my tights over my feet and surrendered to the physical therapists. The physical therapists took my back pain so seriously I went to see them every day. It kept me dancing and it fed me something I was not getting from my teachers or other dancers. But when they could not do enough to stop the pain, they asked me if I'd like to see a doctor. And because my brace was off when they asked me this, I felt unsupported and fragile, and said yes, I thought that would be a good idea. I was ashamed and thrilled to ask for help; although that back injury was not my showstopper, I see now that my back was the part of my body that was most vulnerable and had hurt the most consistently.

The very next day, someone from the school made an appointment and shuttled me to the Boston Children's Hospital. The nurses let me pick the music to listen to during my bone scan, and I picked *The Sound of Music* from their meager selection because it reminded me of movie nights with my brother long ago in London. The doctor had ordered the scan to look for a fracture, which the doctor suspected I had—but it turned up nothing but an unstable sacroiliac joint, the joint that connects the pelvis to the sacrum, and lots of inflammation. With an unstable sacroiliac joint, my pelvis would dislocate every time I took a ballet class to the point where I could not remember where it was supposed to be. I had danced crooked to accommodate it, ignoring or forgetting that it wasn't supposed to hurt so much to dance. "I'd like to see a linebacker play under these conditions," one doctor said, which gratified me.

Although there was no reprieve in the pain, the validation of hearing it really existed was a relief. The white brace would hold in place what my muscles could not. He told me to keep wearing it, not just after class but while I danced. Like all dancers, my mantra was "the show must go on." My injury made me feel weak, and hiding it let me keep up the myth that with a little support, I could pretend I was just as strong, and just as determined to stick it out, as everyone else. It never occurred to me that ballet's logic was flawed—instead I believed my body was.

Each evening, after a long day of classes and rehearsals, we sat with ice packs and counted our blisters. I remember dancers by their injuries. Pointe work made Laura's ankles hurt. Grace's knees got sore from over-turning out. Jessica had a sore rib after her partner had gripped her too tightly in a pirouette.

One evening, much like all the others, we sat around the TV in the common room watching *Indiana Jones,* saying the lines along with Harrison Ford. We named the ways our bodies were imperfect, which we knew by heart—the arches of my feet, Andi's legs, which weren't hyperextended, Claudia's hips, which didn't turn out. And then we comforted each other. Tending to our pain was a collective routine, sitting in a circle in the common room, telling stories of who'd said what and who'd danced how. I felt a deep sense of belonging each humid New England evening. My young pain didn't yet feel like a chronic injury, but a necessary part of pushing myself to dance as beautifully and as fully as I could. In fact, having pain made me feel like I belonged in that circle of hot teenage girl bodies. Now, none of the girls dance anymore. I wish we had known when we were sixteen that summer evening that pain wasn't a sign of bravery. That it wasn't just a necessary grinding of the gears.

The day after my visit to the Children's Hospital, I walked into class with everyone else, and when I got there, the chain-smoking Russian ballet dancer who would make us do 100 relevés per day to bulk the muscles of our calves came to me as I stood stretching at the barre. He, like all ballet dancers, walked with his toes turned out. It was morning, when the whole day still seemed possible. Under my leotard I felt the itch of the brace, and also its promise to hold me up while I threw myself into daily class.

The ballet master asked me to follow him, so we walked outside together, and stood under a tree. "You are not to take class anymore," he said. "We can no longer let you." He delivered this news matter-of-factly as though it was just an errand to him.

"Why?" I asked, surprised that he knew who I was, flattered by what I mistook for his sympathy.

"It is dangerous for us to let you dance with this back injury." His face was set, his arms crossed. Going to the physical therapists after my classes was one thing, but going to the Boston Children's Hospital for a bone scan, it seemed, was quite another. I had thought I'd kept the brace well hidden under my leotard, but with all those eyes on us every day, it was hard to keep secrets about our bodies. That brace comforted me as much as it supported me. But once I decided to take the injury seriously and get it checked out, it seemed I'd broken an unspoken rule. I'd left a record by admitting too much. I tried to argue with him, to tell him I was fine, but I was a child—the doctor must have communicated to the ballet school that I was not, in fact, fine.

In a back office a few minutes later, the director of the summer program told me I was not to dance again that summer. Her walls were covered with black and white posters of famous dancers in rehearsals, their faces concentrated, their limbs wrapped in legwarmers and bands, protecting their muscles and keeping them warm between repetitions. It was the only time all summer the director had spoken to me, the only thing that made her, even for an instant, remember my name. My injury put me on the map.

"I once knew a girl," she told me, "who was injured. She came to every class and sat in the front with a notebook, where she wrote down every correction and every lesson the teacher gave. When she recovered, she danced much better than she did before. Her artistry and her technique had improved just from observing." Observing others was something I loved almost as much as I loved observing my own body in the mirror as it cut diagonals through the humid studio. But it was not the same as learning my body's limitations, nor of finding a new way to reach towards its potential. It did not let me support my own muscles when a brace no longer did it for me.

There is a substantial line between burdening someone else with our retellings of our suffering and admitting it to ourselves, but I didn't know which side of it I stood on. The school had forced me to confess what I thought I should have kept to myself. So I called my parents and told them my back hurt terribly and I wanted to come home. That my body felt quite apart from me, something that held me back from what I wanted. At the same time, it was the only tool I had to express myself. This phone call home felt like defeat, like unbracing myself only to turn into a puddle on the floor. For a full day, I kept that I was going home to myself before I told my gang of friends, worried that without ballet I'd cut the gossamer web that bound us together. Ignoring my back pain that summer, hiding that brace under my clothes, put me at odds with my own body, whose materiality had become a hindrance, something to fix or support, waiting until it healed or took the shape I wanted.

Finally, I flew home early, relieved to let my mother take care of me, because I hadn't yet learned I could do that for myself. It was a final adolescent act that summer: of creating pain, and escaping not only from it, but also from the responsibility of healing it without support from something, or someone, outside of me. Perhaps getting kicked out of ballet camp for an injury would be enough to stop some dancers from putting themselves through that again, but I wasn't ready to let go. I still thought my pain was necessary to the beauty of dancing.

6

Telling the story of my chronic back pain provides signposts and milestones. I can track my growth from one brace to the next. The first brace in Boston felt like restraint. The second brace, after my fall on that California winter night, felt like a bolster. Nothing had changed between those two injuries except me.

In Boston, I had known nothing of myself besides that I was a dancer. By the second time, I knew I was other things as well. I was a few years older by then, and these parallel milestones proved to me that in the intervening years, I began to let some of the rest of the world bleed into mine: the books and cities I loved, the people who saw me as something other than a useful body.

After my showstopper fall in rehearsal when I was nineteen, my knees pulled to my chest, staring at the fluorescent lights as the music kept playing, I knew deep down this pain was so bad I would never be rid of it. But my mind was scrubbed of anything besides panic. I didn't want to move, but I wanted desperately to go to the emergency room to verify what I was feeling, to make sure I was really splintered beyond repair.

That night, I couldn't get to the hospital without help so someone—I've forgotten who—wheeled me in. That was the only thing that seemed at all extraordinary: I sat down in a chair, the chair moved, and suddenly I was in a new place.

Three X-rays were backlit on the wall, and the doctor pointed to them as though I might recognize something in them. Mostly I saw the tree branches of my ribs, white and blurred, like an anatomical equation that I was trying to solve.

"Here's the fracture in the lower spine. L4 and L5 have compressed here and here as well, see this bulge, and the fluid has begun to leak." The doctor used a pen to point, but to me it looked just like it was supposed to.

"Down here is narrowed disc." He traced them in a smooth arc. "This is mostly like the result of years of wear and tear on your spine."

"If you were a normal weight," the doctor added, "You might have had more cushion in your butt. Try to gain a few pounds, okay?"

He was looking at the valleys between my bones, my frail frame and the way my hip bones stuck out because I hadn't eaten a full meal in months. He was looking at the soft downy fuzz that grows on a starving body to keep it warm. But who knows what would have happened if I had more weight on me. If I hadn't danced through the pain so many times before. If every other circumstance were not what it was.

A rheumatologist gave me my diagnosis: the disc between my L6 and L7 lumbar spine was dangerously herniated, and I had torn the ligaments that held my sacrum and ilium bones together, so I could no longer keep my own alignment. He referred me to physical therapy, but I had gone to physical therapy for back pain before, and knew the limits of their understanding of the demands ballet puts on a body. Even the chiropractor I'd seen with my grandmother could only provide me with temporary relief. I'd overestimated my own ability to dance through pain and ended up in almost daily spasms, which the doctor assured me was my body's way of seizing the muscles around the site of injury to prevent further damage. "This is a pain you should listen to," he told me. "You really shouldn't do much of anything as your back relaxes and begins to heal."

"Could I just do barre?" I asked him. Surely barre was safe: only the warmup section and short combinations to prepare for dancing unassisted.

"You shouldn't even walk much while this heals," he replied, writing down my referral for physical therapy. "I want you to lie on a hard surface with lots of pillows under your knees for as long as it takes for the spasms to stop." Before I left, he produced what looked like a big white Ace bandage and pulled up my shirt to show me how to strap myself in.

"This back brace will hold your sacroiliac joint in place until you can relearn to do it yourself," he explained. As he talked, he wrapped the big white bandage around my middle and, using a little metal clip, tugged it in place to hold me together. It was tight and pinched in some places, but wearing it helped me move carefully.

In the car ride back home, I told my parents that while I was injured, maybe I'd try to write, my second favorite thing to do. "Writing hurts in better places," I told them. In my first year of college, worried I was disappearing in my ballet classes, I'd taken a poetry class. I'd loved it—something I was able to wedge in between dance classes that fed me, even as I danced on an empty stomach. The A I earned on my poems made me feel like I had another voice. And that voice would end up saving me.

When we got home to my parents' house from the doctor's office, I lay on the Southwestern rug next to their age-swollen grand piano, and the sunlight dripped through the window beside me as though spilled from a pitcher. Adapting to daily pain is a full-time job that, like any other, becomes as unconscious as a gesture, hair tucked behind an ear, the absent-minded twirl of an earring. Down on the floor, I relearned each movement to minimize the pain until living that way became automated.

From the floor I lost my confidence, my sureness in what my body could accomplish. I became what I was: a body in recline. A body, broken. I grew depressed, and then determined, and then depressed. I told myself I'd just have to sit out for a few weeks until I could dance again, that I was still young enough that my body would bounce back and I'd be able to resume my life without too big of a setback.

I had my parents or my brother help me downstairs where the TV was, where I'd watch old tapes of myself dancing—as the dew-drop fairy in *The Nutcracker* or as Cupid in *Don Quixote* or a sylph in *Les Sylphides*. I watched the great story ballets. I watched the documentary about the young Swedish ballerina who, while doing ronds de jambes at the barre tells the man filming her, *it always hurts somewhere, and just now I feel it in my hip*. I watched the man's solo from American Ballet Theater's *La Bayadère* over and over, marveling at how Ángel Corella, my great love back then, could jump in the air, spin 180 degrees, and fling his legs into a split jump all within a second.

I ran through the choreography in my head from the role I'd been dancing when I fell, and imagined somewhere another girl happily stepping in, glad to be given the opportunity. It was painful to think of my friends still dancing when I couldn't, like a betrayal. I missed the casting for the spring Balanchine ballet, so I listened to the score over and over, wondering when my body would belong to me again, wondering which part I would have gotten and which girl had it instead.

Days before my fall, my roommate back at college, also a dance major, had left her diary open on her desk, a purple pen uncapped in its seam. Without touching it, my boyfriend had leaned over and read, aloud, "She always complains about her back after class. I am so sick of it." I felt the stinging heartfire of criticism, of another person witnessing my pain witheringly, and wanted to call her now and say, "See? It broke! It really did hurt!" My pain felt like walking through a new landscape, senses at attention in a new terrain, everything crowding out everything else's importance. Like visiting a new place, pain made me focus on a small incident to distract me from the more terrifying abstract questions: what would I do if I never healed? Why would I want to dance again if it caused me this much pain?

⚜

The story of the fall in that ballet rehearsal when I was nineteen is the showstopper, but it's not what stopped me from dancing. The years that followed did. Chronic pain is anticlimactic both to the sufferer and an audience: a new landscape no one would choose to visit. No one asks to see your back brace like they do pictures of where you've traveled. No one asks you questions about whether they should go to this new place too, where they should sleep or visit. Instead, chronic pain is isolating—both as I lived it and as I remember it years later. I feel it to this day, especially when I sit for long periods while I read or write.

That kind of recovery left me more time than usual to read, something that I usually did only between class and rehearsal. Now, I could devote the time between injury and recovery to it. I began reading through a book list of great women writers. While my friends back at college were learning new choreography, getting sunburned together on the weekends, I read *Rebecca* and *Lolita*, *Mrs. Dalloway* and *My Antonia*. They were the only thing that allowed me an interior life compelling enough to forget about how my body felt. They gave me a softer landing so I did not splinter when I met the ground. They acted as a much stronger brace than the one I wore around my back. The books I read those months that I healed are still among the most important of my life.

I saw while I read that the roles available to women were far more numerous and distinguished than I'd ever realized, that lives could be exciting without ballet as an escape hatch. Some women didn't need an escape hatch at all. I saw women who cast themselves in the parts they wanted—traveler, public intellectual, part of a community of artists that debated their work, wrote on their own terms, took risks, broke rules. I looked for myself in the pages of each novel I read. I saw women focusing on something other than the size of their bodies. Women in novels like *Madame Bovary* and *The Awakening* would rather not live at all than live in a small, stifled world.

Troy, my physical therapist during that time, was not the first man to teach me how to move, but he was the first one to ask me how it felt. I recognized the massages and exercises from the sessions I'd had in Boston years earlier. He often told me to "listen" to my body, and I rolled my eyes. Pain is telling another story, but you can't hear it if you don't listen to it. I took notes of each movement and where it fell on the pain scale. "Sitting down, 4. Standing up, 6."

Writing, like dancing, was a physical act. After all, isn't every story a story from our bodies, meant to cause a response in someone else's? I'm convinced I wrote my way better, passing the tedious time until I could do all my exercises for Troy without pain. He told me eventually that I was as good as I was going to get. "Just keep listening to your body," he told me.

I knew he was right—that it was only by forming this new muscle memory and testing out each new motion that I could heal—but it's not the way I was used to experiencing my body. The pain of not dancing felt more acute than the pain of my back. I missed being lifted by my partner and told I was light as a feather, the ways I had to mimic love for some boy I barely knew during rehearsals, the thrill of casting lists and late-night rehearsals. I missed stumbling home exhausted from working so hard, and going to bed knowing I'd rehearsed a role that was far more exciting than my own life. Ballet was always my greatest adventure, and my greatest connection both to myself and to the people I danced with. I didn't yet trust how I felt, and so I tried to listen a little closer to the story I heard from my body.

Dancing is a constant vanishing point, over as soon as it materializes, after all those months and years of preparation. When I could not dance, I worried that it was not just the dance, but me who had begun to vanish. So I wrote things down, to leave traces of myself around the house: to-do lists, recipes, and plans for my future. All the stories my body told me.

What I felt now was a sort of more aching pain after a long day, the spasms happening only once a month, then twice a year, then every other year. The pain is a reminder of the happiness of a neat tour jeté and a soft landing, the impossibility of perfection, and pain's permanent residence in my nervous system and muscle memory, from heart to toes, from spine to brain. The leftover pain is a reminder that my body isn't done telling its story, nor am I done writing it. So I got up, sat in a chair, and tried to write down the things I'd read and thought about down on the floor.

Getting up allowed me to go back to school. It was spring quarter by the time I returned to college, but I didn't enroll in any ballet classes, since I was still in pain; I looked into creative writing. By fall, I knew I wanted to go to Paris and experience something bigger than a rehearsal studio. I still loved ballet, but my life had cleaved in two, and I knew the seismologic rupture inside me meant I could never risk fully sacrificing my body in the name of art again. Looking back it's clear I was packing my bags and keeping them by the front door, slightly ajar, the car motor running. After all, there were other things to fall in love with too.

I worried about gaining weight without daily classes, so to compensate I starved myself, eating only an apple when I felt like I might faint. During the time I was back at school but wasn't dancing, I lost twenty pounds over the course of a month and a half. My clothes were baggy, but hiding beneath them made me feel safer. Why would I want to show off a body that had betrayed me so dramatically? I'd punish myself for eating meals, spending hours on the elliptical machine, reading for my classes or for pleasure. Once, at a party, I heard one girl whisper to another, "She is so skinny it's disgusting." I looked down at the concave space between my ribs and hip bones, proud I stood out in some way. "They're just jealous," I told myself. When my weight was about ninety-five pounds, I'd cry myself to sleep. "That is unacceptable," I'd whisper. The next day, I wouldn't put anything into my body except watermelon and tea. I refused to nourish the body that kept me away from ballet. I had always been suspicious of food, terrified of any weight on my tiny frame, but the obsession with restricting food fully replaced my obsession with ballet, and gave me some sense of control over a body that seemed completely beyond my will.

⚜

Injury has, on the surface, two possible outcomes—one in which we overcome the injury and return to our lives as they were, and one that stops us altogether, forces us to pivot, to learn how to live with chronic pain. I wasn't yet sure which ending my story would have, because I didn't know I could write the ending myself. I stopped dancing because it caused me pain, but I still remember the joy and power that dancing once gave me. There is a third possible outcome from injury: one that would let me heal enough to dance again, but not without pain, forcing me to choose every day how much I will push through the pain to do the thing I loved so much.

One of my best friends in college told me, after reading some of my writing in class during that time when I was not dancing, that she could tell I'd never been in love. "But I have," I wanted to say, "with ballet." By then, though, it was beginning to feel like a love whose name I was forgetting. I wish I could say I never danced again, that I had finally realized how I'd been complicit in my body's pain, but endings are never so neatly tied up. I was ready to look beyond ballet, but I wasn't yet ready to leave it completely behind me.

7

Looking back, I remember all the ways ballet hurt me, but I still remember the joy and power of dancing that came first. And yet, it was only after I made a small slice of space in my life for something else that the blurred edges of new options came into sharper focus. I thought that my injury would not be the end of my dancing as long as I could write about it.

I had begun taking French classes in high school to help me with the language of ballet, the first of my two lives. I named the steps my body could do, the whispered rush of canvas shoes against the linoleum floors, that spot between clavicles that pulsed with both breath and heartbeat, the joints swollen like trapped marbles. I assumed, when it came time to pick a foreign language, that learning French would bring me closer to myself by bringing me closer to the dancing that consumed me. It did, and it brought me more than I could ever have imagined.

By college, French classes gave me the same feeling of watching a life that wasn't mine, up close, like I was an audience member of someone else's life. I saw the way French people had arguments, played practical jokes, picked out the radishes for their dinner. It felt like a show that existed for my delight. I was hooked. To study abroad at the Sorbonne Nouvelle in Paris, I just had to pass a quick language exam, get clearance from my doctor, and, most difficult of all, say goodbye to my parents and brother for a year. I still remember the hitch in my father's voice as he told me he loved me at LAX. I watched him grow smaller as I drifted up the escalator to security. The string that connected our two hearts stretched taut as I ventured off on my own.

I read about other women's lives, perhaps as a way to study my own obsessions and aspirations from a distance. My reading in those days often centered around muses, the women who orbited geniuses, feeding and inspiring them and only to have their own names erased from the annals of artists' mythos. Their erasure reminded me of what it felt like to devote my whole life to something and then, abruptly, stop, leaving no trace.

Lucia Joyce, the daughter of James Joyce, and Zelda Fitzgerald, the wife of F. Scott Fitzgerald, began ballet in their early twenties, about the time I admitted to myself that I needed to stop. Both women were institutionalized for madness. What is it about dance, I wondered, that felt like a fever dream, an ecstasy—the possessed Red Shoes or the spirits in "Giselle" that made the prince dance until his own death? What was it about dance that felt like it required all of me, or nothing at all? What had kept these women from jumping from the highest window they could find?

Lucia Joyce, I read, danced around her father as he wrote. He believed he could cure her madness if only he finished *Finnegans Wake*. He allowed her, according to one of her cousins, to dance silently in the background while he worked on his linguistic abstractions that make up that novel. Carol Loeb Shloss wrote, in her biography of Lucia Joyce, "The writing of the pen, the writing of the body became a dialogue of artists, performing and counterperforming, the pen, the limbs writing away." Lucia Joyce had begun taking dance lessons much later than I had, at age fifteen, from Isadora Duncan's brother; her mother became jealous of the attention she received dancing onstage at a time when that was considered unseemly. After a series of breakdowns, her family committed her to an insane asylum in Ivry, outside Paris, and rarely spoke of her again. Her father, however, maintained that despite committing her, she was not crazy but an artistic co-conspirator. It was not a rupture in her body, but her mind, that put an end to the great love she would always mourn: ballet.

Joyce's grandson, now the protector of his literary legacy, has successfully sued biographers of the family to remove chapters on Lucia before publication. Her erasure is ongoing, complete and unsettling. By keeping silent about Lucia, her family allowed her father to feed on her dancing and her madness and then erase her from history. I'd misunderstood the role of the muse, seeing it as flattering, instead of a way for artists to test the unique challenges of their art forms at the expense of a young woman's body. Just like ballet.

The realization that she would never be the dancer she wanted to be broke Joyce. Dance, just like language, was imperfect and limited. Lucia's name is only recognizable to most people because of her father, whose writing outlasts her. Biographers might implicate the illnesses of their minds, rather than the fragility of their bones, as the fissure that never healed.

I spent the first five months of my year in Paris sitting in literature classes with an American boy in my program I'd fallen in love with—I loved him for his energy in exploring a new city together and the way he made fun of himself, and spent our classes together passing notes and doodles.

In a class at the Sorbonne that year we read books that taught me, among other things, that waiting for men to save me, like the heroes of classical ballet, wasn't my only option. In a 19th-century French realism class, I read and wrote long essays in French about women who tried desperately to save themselves, Emma Bovary and Eugénie Grandet. I read Colette and saw what was possible for women who wanted to write. My literature professor came up to me after class and said, in front of the boy, "You've written a very good argument in your last essay. Can I read it aloud to the class tomorrow?" I told him of course, and the next day, when he read it, he told the class, "Excuse any grammar mistakes, but this was written by someone whose native language is not French." As he read it, I sat there, listening to my own words in a foreign language, my whole body quivering. The class discussed my essay when the professor was done. But my strongest memory of that day was my sadness that the boy I had a crush on was not in the room; he might never know I was smart. I was more disappointed by his absence than I was proud of my writing.

The French took to the streets so often, I was infected with the spirit of being loud, taking up space, of using my body as more than a way to move through the world around me. I learned I could use it for love too, for sitting beside another body in the back seat of a car, hoping for excuses to press together.

It was months after my major fall, but I wasn't as happy to dance as I was to walk miles and miles around Paris with new friends. One of my classmates, still a dear friend to this day, invited me to West African dance lessons with her. We stood in a circle and learned new rhythms. For the first time in my life I felt my hips move when I danced, and how natural that felt. After those classes, out of habit, I stayed for ballet classes, grateful the language was the same as it was back home. But moving across the world only to end up in a ballet studio depressed me. It looked like any studio I could have danced in back home. Still, I found some comfort in my new freedom to drop in for a class and then not show up the next day if my back was sore. No one was counting on me to be there. In fact, no one seemed to care whether I danced or not.

That year, I fed my hunger in a boy's chambre de bonne: a plate of coq au vin, a meal he cooked for me, a gesture I misread as love. I was so hungry for food that I didn't notice if I was unfed in other ways. I'd toyed for years with hunger, keeping it close in case I needed it, fingering its fringe, staving off any changes to my body should they ever occur. The year in France facilitated a transformation in how I thought about my body, and the importance of feeding and caring for it.

The old woman I lived with taught me to make ratatouille by telling me to throw in whatever might rot soon. It made me pay attention to decay, to see it in the wrinkled skin of a tomato, and to feel it in my own body. Ballet, like any demanding movement, makes the body break down, but our denial of our own pain speeds the process up.

⟳

Then my first heartbreak—which I dove into with reckless, upside-down abandon—and my first car accident, which happened concurrently. It felt like taking a leap onto a dark stage, hoping to land in my partner's arms, only I hit the ground and crumpled, that old pain spreading from the bottom of my spine to the top. That year in Paris, I found myself, one last time, in a brace. It would be the only one I ever wore that had nothing to do with ballet, and it was the one that helped me the most.

Everybody said they had known it was coming. We were somewhere in Provence at dusk, and I had been looking in my lap when
the other car came towards us, thinking about the Left Bank until
the moment of impact. We spun around twice before I even knew
what was happening. My neck jolted so that the pain in my back
ignited in a long and uninterrupted flame from the tip of my tail-
bone to the bottom of my skull. I called out in surprise, and my
boyfriend took my hand as we crashed. After the cars collided, we
slid backwards down an embankment. Just moments before, I had
seen the ocean for the first time since summer. It wasn't the same
ocean from home in California, green and mirroring, full of kelp
and clouds and sunlight. It was gray and reminded me of looking
down a hole whose bottom I couldn't see.

In the car's spin, I made a choice without knowing it, to steel
myself against what was happening or to lean into it. I chose the
first option, like I had done so many times before.

Immediately after the accident, as I listened to the police talk
to the two drivers, I heard my friend who had been driving say she
almost turned the wheel in time to avoid the collision. It was a new
phrase to me, this "almost." In French, it sounded like a close call, a
falter, of nearly regaining balance. I began to use it often as I healed,
and the words in French took on a gravity that seemed fitting for
the event. *J'ai failli.*

It all felt like a sign—hearing a ballet word, new to me, in the
French countryside at dusk after a car accident, and realizing the
conversations I could have now that I had the words: *I almost ate
dinner. I almost didn't hurt my back in ballet. I almost chose another life.*

A *failli* is a ballet step as well, one whose meaning I'd never
thought to look up. A dancer doing a failli tries to degage each leg
to the front, one immediately after the other, with a small jump. It's

an in-between step, a precursor to a big jump. I later heard a teacher define it as "giving way."

Learning how to say *faillir*—what I'd almost done—split me in half. Now that I had a word for it, the whole world seemed a series of near misses. I realized all the things that could go wrong and didn't, and the things that could have gone right but instead left me standing in Provence at dusk, broken again. The word let me see my parallel life: the one in which I had never fallen, the one in which I had never danced at all.

In the collision, my boyfriend's head had struck against something, and his tooth had bitten through the skin of his mouth and chipped, ever so slightly. He was fine, though. Although I am not proud of this, I wished he were injured, just a little, so that he wouldn't be able to leave me there in France and go back home to California. I was staying the year, and he was only staying that semester. I wished I were hurt too, enough for him to feel worried, and to mistake that worry for love. But I was young; how could I have known how to love the way adults should? That's what we learn through loving the wrong people, the wrong ways, and through being loved the wrong ways too.

Looking at that boyfriend in the December cold, as we waited for an ambulance, the air was bitter and windy. It was difficult to recognize our car from what remained. It had been forced from its body, had broken to form a new distorted shape that resembled a car but was not a car. We took small sips of salty air and our noses ran in the chilly night air. Slowly we unfolded, still unsure for another few moments what our bodies would do, but we learned they would stand, and we learned they felt best when pressed together in the cold as we waited for someone to come save us from this embankment.

For some reason, when I try to conjure the scenery around us that day to set it down in writing, a stretch of the highway in my hometown in California comes to mind. The pain of my neck after my car crash in Provence must have gotten conflated in my memory with the pain in my back after years of ballet. Parts of the spine and highways at dusk blur together.

J'ai failli. It was only a day trip, something we could have just as easily skipped, an in-between step, a precursor to the real movement. I was learning, through the process of healing my back, studying French literature, eating food, or falling in love, to consider more of myself than just my body, or else to consider all the things a body could do when it was not dancing.

I was glad the car accident had bought us extra time before the boyfriend went back home without me, and in some way, bonded us together in a memory of one really bad day of our lives. When he had told me the day before the accident that he didn't want to be my boyfriend while I remained in Paris, I thought I could change his mind with the very strength of my beating heart.

The next day, after he had left, I would go to a local doctor, who would put me in a neck brace for a month and a half. "You were in the whiplash seat," the doctor would tell me, "the second seat of impact." This was a form of impact that everyone could plainly see. I was going through a first pathetic heartbreak invisibly, but the neck brace so obviously signaled pain that at least I was not starved for the validation I always sought.

When the exchange program heard I had been in a car accident, the director called and asked me to come back to Paris. He picked me up at the train station and took me to his house, where his wife cooked me dinner. He offered to cut up my sausage, which I let him do not because my neck hurt, but because my heart did, and it felt good to let someone take care of me. My vocabulary expanded in the American Hospital he took me to, where, it turned out, they didn't speak English. Do not swallow or breathe, a woman's automated voice told me each time they took an MRI. *Ne pas avaler, ni respirer.* Brace yourself, she seemed to tell me.

One way I braced myself was by avoiding ballet, the cause of so much physical pain that I associated it with the pain from the car accident too. I stopped going to either West African dance or ballet classes once I returned to Paris, the first time I'd ever stopped dancing without a doctor telling me explicitly I had to. I stopped simply because my spine hurt, and because I was so in love with the streets of Paris. I went other places that demanded less of me in some ways, and much more of me in others. Instead of dancing, I filled my time doing things I couldn't have done back home, looking through Père Lachaise to find Abelard and Héloïse's graves, or sipping kir royales in the basement at Pop In on rue Amelot. I learned all the things I could do when I wasn't struggling to dance through chronic injury. I took long walks, made friends I love to this day, ate French pastries in parks, went to concerts and bars and the catacombs. I went to a museum every single week with my French history classes. I read French novels and British ones. I spent several weeks in Sicily with a wonderful family whose daughter I'd met when she'd studied abroad in California. She took me all over the Sicilian coast. Her parents, who spoke not a word of English, made me elaborate home-cooked meals and took care of me with the most kindness I've ever experienced. I began writing notes for what eventually turned into this book.

Vague plans to keep writing took a firmer shape in my head in France. I knew I had something to say that required words rather than my body. I decided I would apply to MFA programs in writing once I got back to California. I did my research, asked my professors for letters of recommendation. I started and stopped and started again, several essays I thought I could use as a sample. I didn't realize then what a cliché it was to be so transformed by my junior year of college study abroad, but as I learned self-sufficiency, I learned to individuate not only from my familiar culture and family, but from ballet, which had a greater hold on me than anything else.

◦⊱❀⊰◦

Unbracing, and giving way, is the important second step of being braced, allowing a joint to falter, a first love to go, words to stop short of what I want to say. It means making room for something bigger, about to come, while still naming and honoring the failli, the in-between steps. I will always be grateful I didn't dance the year I was in France because of all the other things I did instead.

When that brace came off, I relearned the kinks and stickiness of my own muscles. All bodies have limitations, even in youth, even for dancers, who move far more and far bigger than most lives allow, who dance until they are hurt beyond bargaining and barely notice until they limp home. At some point, though, the brace must come off. I had to be strong enough to stand back up, and by then, I was.

Before that final brace in France, I had never really learned to hold myself up. But this time, I discovered something new about myself: wearing a neck brace for six weeks hadn't felt like a barrier from doing what I loved. Without dance, the brace no longer held me back, which also meant I no longer needed it to keep me together.

My original injury had begun in the joint between my sacrum and iliac, held in place by the strongest ligaments in the human body. The car accident moved it to my cervical spine, the gateway to my head. There are ways our minds and our bodies speak to one another. Even my strongest joints cannot support me, so instead, I'd have to learn the ways to brace against instability. When the treatment is invisible—an injection, exercises, a brace under a shirt or a leotard—I am forced to hunt around for words to describe how I make allowances for my body. And like everyone, I want to be seen. I had hidden my pain before, but now, with a visible neck brace, I could not hide. Instead, I accepted people's help, and learned to help myself.

A brace supports us only so long as our muscles can't. The muscles eventually have to relearn, or remember, how to hold us up. In the same way, I had to learn how to hold myself up without ballet, and without the dreams I developed as a dancer. Maybe the physical jolt in my neck after the car accident was a way to beg my mind to pay attention to what was happening down below it, to stop dancing if it made my body break down faster. Maybe the accident was not the near miss—ballet was. After all, I almost didn't stop dancing.

8

Back in California, a friend asked me to visit her at the eating disorder clinic she had been committed to. Buried in my decision to take her up on her invitation was a tacit acknowledgement that I had been where she now was and had come out on the other side.

So one Sunday afternoon, I took a drive down the spine of California and then cut inland, where I passed through dry brown hills.

The landscape was a hotter, emptier place than the coast. There, I found a graceless building where I parked and went inside to visit Annabel. She was climbing the mountain of anorexia and I was there half out of a sense of duty and half out of a belief that there was anything I could do to help. Annabel knew I had climbed the same mountain years earlier, and I wished I could tell her what was on the other side. I wished I could tell her it took reading books and going to Paris. I wish I could tell her it never leaves your brain completely but it gets easier to eat if you try.

I signed my name in the visitor's book as she came around the corner, hair brushed, face made up, and took me outside "so we can talk." She had called it a trailer park in her emails, but it was a permanent structure—the ugliest building in a nice neighborhood. We hadn't seen each other in four years, but she sat down with me as though we had just left off a familiar conversation.

"These other girls," she said, and rolled her eyes. "Oh my god."

We were sitting in a cheerless patio, and there was a flowerpot next to her chair filled with cigarette butts. After each sentence, she looked to me for approval, but I was trying to pretend I was someone I wasn't: serene, wise, on the mountaintop. This meant making the face my mother made in photos when she was younger—a very convincing half-smile.

"What's wrong with them?" I asked, but I knew what she meant. I saw the girls through the windows, lying on couches in sweatpants, and knew how unimpressed Annabel must be.

"Two of them were in the military," Annabel told me, as though this was something we could both agree was insufferable.

When I had last seen Annabel, she was a young teenager and I babysat for her family in New York, spending most of my time trying to stop her younger brother from sneaking candy before the housekeeper gave him dinner. I knew why Annabel was miserable in treatment. She was away from college and her family's Fifth Avenue apartment. Away from the parties in New York and the vacations to Europe. Her letters had been an intricate patchwork of vulnerability and optimism, but in person I saw she was wearing thin. She hated the other girls almost as much as she hated herself.

In our correspondence over the last few months, she told me how sick she was. I tried to stack my own past up against hers. Somewhere along the way it became clear that Annabel had taken this much further than I ever had, and during our correspondence I became aware that I was competing with her, matching story for story, calorie for calorie, until I told myself I should try to lose this game. I knew, for example, that this was Annabel's second treatment center in California. She was kicked out of the first one—a much nicer place where celebrities go, because she bragged about purging and "it triggered the other girls." I knew she was asked to take an indefinite leave from college and that her parents didn't know what else to do when she didn't stop purging or working out once she got home to New York. Now she was in California, and I had promised to visit. What was she shrinking from? What space did she not want to inhabit?

We talked for only a minute about her college friends who started going to the dining commons without her every day. "No one knows how to handle it," I told her, but I could see she was angry with them and I was speaking into the wind. I had felt just as cut off from my own friends my first year of college, and maybe the fact that I had never spoken to any of them again was a way of punishing them for what I had been doing to myself.

Annabel showed me how she had carved into her feet with anything sharp she could find. She was wearing sandals, and I'd already noticed the scars. I'd also noticed the eroding enamel on her teeth, but we were pretending those still looked healthy.

"They won't let me have a closet door," she told me. "I used to be upstairs in a different room, but I threw up every night in the closet. On the carpet," she added.

"You're proud of this, aren't you?" I asked.

"Yeah!" she said. I could almost remember my pride in my own hunger.

"The staff here doesn't trust me," she said. "I'm on twenty-four-hour observation. I have to sleep downstairs with a nurse and I can't shower or pee by myself." She said she sees herself getting fat. When I responded, I felt like I saw my own former body-terror out of the corner of my eye: a teenager, leaning against the wall.

But Annabel was already on to the next story: their daily outings to the park, where she wasn't allowed to walk.

"They make me sit on a yoga mat, but sometimes I find reasons to get up, like today I saw a little boy who needed help, so I ran over and did the monkey bars with him," she told me.

The question I wanted to ask her, but didn't, was what had made her feel like she needed to disappear. I wondered if she'd experienced trauma, or whether the assault was the gradual chipping away at her self-worth as she transitioned into womanhood.

❦

Before ballet class in high school, I used to watch the older girls pile their hair up on their heads with their pale fingers, letting it fall a few times before securing it with pins. I sat watching this over many years, in a corner of a rehearsal room while the class before finished their grand allegro, or in the long dark hallways, all in silence. I sat in the splits, even though I had been warned not to stretch before class, before the muscles we warmed up through repetitions of small circular movements, the warmth starting at the ankle and moving up the body as though we were climbing in a body of water.

Still, stretching in front of the other girls was a way of showing what you could do before you even stood up. Before we could move for each other, we silently bragged by laying on our backs and stomachs and fanning our legs around us. We bragged with our feet, with our shoulders. We bragged with our knees.

Then I went to college and became a dance major and sat in dance studios there too.

"Orange and green foods should always be paired together. Red food is the best. I avoid yellow food altogether, at least before dinner." My friend Emma said that to me. As she spoke, I pictured my hip bones jutting like ledges for my elbows to rest on. We had just begun college, still immune from the world, where our time stretched ahead like a yawn.

I had begun to eat things in groups of eight. I chewed eight times, ate only eight slices of a banana. I didn't tell her this, though. I hadn't yet noticed it, hadn't yet looked on it with clarity.

"You're weird," I said instead.

She massaged her fashion model ankles, and I realized without knowing it that she was beautiful in a way that mattered.

"You take the smallest bites of anyone I have ever seen," she told me calmly. "You eat like a baby bird."

Sitting with Emma before a class or rehearsal, I noticed she was never quite still, that she always seemed to sway and writhe under my watchful gaze. I wondered if this burned more calories.

Yet once we began dancing, there was a lovely deliberateness to her steps, as though she had planned them out before she began moving.

"I want a nap and a chocolate bar," I said to her.

"How can you eat chocolate before you dance? I want a nap and a salad."

"No you don't," I said. "No one wants a salad."

"Mmm, I love them," she told me absently while tying her pointe shoes. She had divided into two halves. One half of her was caught in shadow while the other half glowed in the light of late afternoon.

Once my friend and I moved from the hallway to the studio, we stood at the barre with our legs up on the highest rung. We were eighteen, heads close the way young girls talk. The evening began to soften, and our talk grew tight around us. There were so many small confessions taking place in that room before the teacher came in. Any moment the wisp of a teacher would clap her hands, stand in first position, and gesture to the pianist to begin something slow on the tinny piano. For now, though, we rubbed the taut muscles of our legs and looked closely at each other, speaking with the kinds of smiles people wear when they are discussing things that matter.

Once we began our first combination, the teacher went to each of us, stopping to offer up a light touch with the pad of her finger, placing them on the visible bones of our bodies. This college dance studio was enormous, and could fit so many girls it was easy to get lost. In front of me a girl did a forward bend, and the teacher walked by, barely nodding. When I bent forward the bones of my butt stuck out, and the teacher traced her eyes over the protrusions, and recognized me as one of her own.

"Lovely," she told me. I danced on, full of my own promise. With the curve of her gaze, she had given me permission. Even now, I have never been prouder. If I couldn't be the best in the room, I could at least be the thinnest, which, in ballet, I thought could hide what I lacked in technique. It was the day I must have learned how to stand up taller and throw my shoulders back, to know how good it felt to have someone else plant their expectations in me.

When I was average weight, I was an average dancer. When I was shrinking, I was noticed, and when I was noticed, I got the attention I was born wanting. The equation was flawed, but at the time, nothing seemed simpler or truer.

My parents didn't say anything, although years later, none of us could understand why. Maybe they were too close and couldn't zoom out to see the whole frame. My aunt talked to my mom about my shrinking size, but my mom pointed out I had always been tiny, even as a child, and besides, I was dancing so much. And like any addiction, I was good at hiding, saving up all my calories for the one meal I knew I had to eat in front of other people. On one family vacation, I remember getting up at five in the morning to walk for two hours before anyone else was awake. I made plans around mealtimes so I had an excuse to be gone. I told my family, and myself, that everything was fine.

Hilde Bruch wrote in *The Golden Cage* that starving ourselves is an act of self-assertion for women. Through shrinking, we can enact the terrible loss of control women inherited as soon as we were born, the conflict we face, the needs we hide. By controlling every bite we put in our mouths, and every step we take to work it off, to punish ourselves for taking care of our own hungers, our own weaknesses, our own humanness.

You can fake a lot of things, I knew, but you can never fake ballet. We outlined our chest bones with eyeliner before shows so that they would pop from a distance. We kept secrets from each other religiously, even in the dorms and dining commons where our lives pressed up against each other and secrets seemed impossible. We were never frightened of sprains or aches, humidity or crowded streets or endless Chopin nocturnes. Here was my hope: that one day I would come back so that I could understand what I had left behind.

⌒❧⌐

Before this visit to Annabel at the treatment facility, when I was twenty years old, I sat in an undershirt in my doctor's air-conditioned office. She had a checklist in front of her.

"Do you smoke?" My doctor asked.

"No."

"Drink?"

"Not really," I said.

"I'm putting down that you have an eating disorder," she said. I watched as her pen carved the word "anorexia" into the form, and this stole the breath from me. It was the first time anyone had ever said the word to my face, although friends and family had talked around it for years.

"Really?" I asked her. My eyes traced a bleak line to her face, but I could not read what was written on it.

"I can't in good conscience write that you don't have an eating disorder," she said. Part of me was actually proud she took my pain seriously. After all, with a nameless back injury, isn't that what I'd wanted all along—a word to say, this is what we call the thing that hurts you? The doctor was matter-of-fact, as though diagnosing an ear infection. The room was quiet and breezy, one window open to a quiet parking lot outside, and she scribbled notes as though no one's life had changed at all.

Just like that, there was a definition for me. This word had a morbid heart, but rather than sink deeper into it, I took the health form from her, handed it in to the office in my new college, and flew to Paris. I spent a year there living on the bright edges of the native world, never allowed fully inside.

⚜

Sometimes the boy I loved in Paris and I would leave halfway through class to go to the rue Mouffetard to eat baguettes. Focusing on him distracted me enough to start eating again. One of my American classmates put a picture of me online, taken my first month in Paris, sitting on the banks of the Seine, laughing. My arms are lifted up and my shirt is showing my stomach. "Maybe it's the angle, but she looks hella skinny," someone commented under the picture. My classmate responded, "She's a ballerina." That satisfied anyone who noticed the story my body was telling about my hunger.

One afternoon, as the French autumn was on the verge of turning, the boy sat across my bedroom from me. He was saying something about how men love the soft stomachs of women, the animal warmth of them, and I decided, enough. Dusk clicked into place right as I came up for air. I ate from then on, and loved my soft stomach too, watching its form take shape in his eyes. Once I started eating, I realized all the things I had been hungry for all along.

These are the memories—a doctor who spoke the right words, and a boyfriend abroad too—I kept to myself. They show the outlines of what I'm made of. Each day I kept my body small, it was all I had. What it took to heal was to think about more interesting things than my body—the Pantheon, for example, or Père Lachaise, the pale pink dress in a store window, a perfume I sprayed on my wrist and lifted to smell, the graduate schools I could apply to. By realizing I could think of other powers I had, I eventually forgot my obsession, and slowly healed. How sad it would have been to have ignored Père Lachaise while I counted my steps through it instead, or regretted the breakfast I had enjoyed in a café. How full life seemed when my stomach was full, and my mind too.

For many years my body was not my own: ballet made it belong to everyone who watched. Women learn this over and over and over, in new and surprising ways: the public nature of our bodies, the impact of learning we exist for another's gaze. Our bodies are discussed every day on the news, appear in billboards and magazines, become passive, property, beautiful only when deemed so. It is hard to believe we are worth more than our weight, and sometimes impossible not to. Our bodies are grabbed on subways, our bellies are touched when they carry babies, commented on as we walk by an audience on the street. I grew up on stage, in front of mirrors, learning my body was not my own, but the teacher's, the audience's, my partner's. Rather than fight my body, or transcend it, I learned the ways we control our bodies, and the ways we never can. Starvation made me weak—it contributed to my injury, which contributed to my terrors about my own safety. It was a natural groove to fall into, and to scoop myself back out required that I heal all of the things that had hurt me in ballet.

Women know they might be called on to give their bodies away someday, to grow life from scratch and, if we're lucky, from love. There are an infinite number of ways the female body is a home for someone else: for eyes, for shame, for babies, for sex. For love, and love, and love.

I was not allowed to sit with Annabel while she ate, so I went to the street outside and looked down at my legs, wrapped in summer air. After she ate, Annabel went to see the nurse, where she was probably weighed. She'd told me earlier in the day that they weighed her every morning and after each meal, but never told her the number on the scale. She wasn't allowed to drink excessive amounts of water before weigh-ins, but she found this unreasonable, since she was thirsty when she first woke up. I remembered avoiding water before I weighed myself each morning to decide what kind of day I was worthy of having.

After her mealtime, I went back inside the treatment center and asked where Annabel was. She came back to the dining room table where I sat waiting to say goodbye.

"I didn't finish my dinner so they want me to supplement with soy milk because I'm allergic to Ensure," she told me. Her words belonged to this new vocabulary in which "supplement" was a verb and "Ensure" was a brand. Although I was on the other side of this struggle against shrinking, Annabel's control of her food had shifted the power to her. I was left performing, pretending, while feeling uncomfortable about how much this visit had exposed me to myself.

I sat across from her and watched as she swirled the soy milk around in her glass and took a small sip. Another young woman sat with us and I didn't know whether to pretend she wasn't there. A fed-up woman washed the dishes in the next room. I could tell Annabel was tallying up the number of secret sit-ups she would have to do later in her room. She did these after her roommate was asleep, in the fifteen-minute intervals between when the night nurse (in treatment speak this was the "noc shift") poked her head in the room. The girls weren't allowed to close their bedroom doors, and all bathrooms were locked.

⁂

It didn't simply occur to me to stop eating—everything supported that choice. Nor did it simply occur to me to begin again. I had to find a reason to eat—a boyfriend who said he loved my stomach's softness, books that required my concentration, and life that demanded I be here, fully present for it. In order to write this book, and all the fragments and thoughts I wrote in preparation, I need the mental space that I used to devote to counting calories. Eating is a revolutionary act. Because I eat, I write. Because I eat, I overcome the forces that make me think I should lose ten pounds, that keep me ashamed and shrinking. I learn that growing back from hunger is, for a woman, the greatest form of protest.

9

The year I returned from France to finish college, as I waited for acceptance letters from grad schools, I stood in the wings, behind heavy curtains the color of the night sky. It was a sort of homecoming, and the last time I would dance onstage, but I didn't know that then. As the music started, I tried to run through the whole ballet in my mind before I took a step. But once I began to dance, my muscles would remember what my mind could not.

Backstage I shook my hands as though they were wet and I had no towel. I wished my Mita were sitting in the audience. If she were still alive she would be at every performance. She liked the intrigue of what was happening backstage. She liked knowing secrets about the dancers, and I always told them to her.

As I waited in the wings I thought about the small dramas of the people in the audience. Some of these people might have been on a date, or felt the promise of the evening, knowing anything could happen during a live performance. Some of them were bored by the program they were reading while the house lights were on, or were falling in or out of love at that very second. Some of them were grieving for a person they once knew but were now forgetting, even their faces, even their hands, even their voices. All of those people would watch me as I danced.

A man in a tuxedo sat at a grand piano a few feet from me, and he began playing Ravel. I would have to enter in front of him a few seconds later, and I began to count down. I was small and bare in my green costume, and inside my shoes, my toes were beginning to bleed.

Many tricks exist to ballet; one trick is that the dancer must only look perfect from the angle that people see. The biggest trick is to forget everything she has ever learned. The man in the tuxedo swayed on his bench, and his graceful hands on the keys curved like a woman's spine. Unless you were very close to him, as I was, you almost could not see the way he inhaled in time to what he played. This dance would last for no more than eight minutes, but at the end it felt like I had said something complete. The thought is not mine, but it was entrusted to me for the evening, and in all my bareness I said it, silently, under a spotlight.

I began to dance, my legs naked and sinewy. With my body, I narrated a small story to lots of people without thinking. It wasn't thoughtless, though, that dance. It was the most eloquence I'd managed all day. But my mind quieted while my body spoke. I only concentrated when it was something hard, like a pirouette or a long balance, and when I briefly remembered how little time I had left to dance something so precise.

Sometimes I said a small prayer to St. Francis, to my grandmother, to the vast way the theater opens up so tall that I could only imagine the ceiling.

My mother and father and brother were in the audience that night, and my friends from my past and those from my present. My father was proud of me, but he would not say so, I knew. The first time I performed in pointe shoes, my grandmother told me my father had tears in his eyes, and said to her afterwards, "Wasn't she beautiful!" He did not say that to me, but it's nice to know he felt it and said so.

In the audience was also someone I let kiss me two nights earlier. The first thing he ever asked me was if I was a ballerina, a word no dancer would ever use. He asked me this at a party where I wore a red dress, and then asked if he could take me to a ballet someday soon. As I danced, I could feel him drinking me in with his eyes. Around me, small pools of spotlight dappled the ground, and the music grew soft.

Some small miracles emerged that night, too. Some might say a perfectly rational explanation existed, that adrenaline fueled my dance. I would rather forget all about science and believe in magic, though. In my back were those two vertebrae that had pinched and ruptured. It was miraculous that they felt like nothing while I performed, better than air, like the piano music completed the bones of my spine by resting in them.

Ravel wrote music that looked like wind chimes if you could see it, and tasted like raspberries if it had a taste. In this piece, I was a vision in a man's dream at the seaside a long time ago. In the dream a handsome man in blue sees me and lifts me as though I weigh nothing. When he runs over and spins me around, my legs are in attitude devant and derrière, like a pinwheel on either side of him. When we practiced, he told me not to jump as he spun me because I was so light it was hard to keep my legs from flying away from him with the force of the turn's momentum. Even not jumping into his arms became automatic—I learned to be heavy to let him lift me, anchoring his turn with more weight.

Two other women are on that beach with us: one in orange, one in purple. I am in green. I had danced this piece a few times by then, and I was always the dancer in green. The one who danced in orange kept her thumbs up, chugging her arms like a train, her head thrown back like she was looking for clouds in the sky. The one in purple seemed flirtatious, the most mature of us all.

When Mita was my age she took bullfighting lessons. I don't know anyone else who has fought a bull. I imagine her with satin gleaming and legs straight and squeezed together, ready to spring. This dance is with a bull rather than a man, but like me, she would have to consider when to jump, how to distribute her weight, how quick and light she needed to be. It sounds much more difficult than ballet. The calls she would have had to make would be instinctual, split second. I wonder whether she, too, felt the audience's gaze as they watched her. I wonder if this is something she passed down to me, or whether all women know what it's like to have eyes follow their movement, and to make invisible adjustments accordingly.

Since I didn't fully know it was my last night on stage, all that mattered during those few minutes was how much I could defy gravity. In the dressing room before the show my mother called me and told me there was a large white envelope from Sarah Lawrence College at our house, addressed to me.

"What does it say?" I asked. I knew big envelopes were auspicious.

"It says, 'Congratulations! This is the big envelope!'"

Backstage I whispered to the other girls in the dressing room. "I got into grad school. I'm going to New York!" The plan I'd made for myself in France was finally coming to fruition. This acceptance letter was the affirmation I needed that I was good at something besides ballet, and the permission I needed to leave my old life behind, at least for a while. I thought I might come back to it, that writing might be a plan B or something to do while my back healed. The other dancers gathered around me and hugged me and one of

them even squealed because she knew how much I had wanted
to go, and how nervous I had been that I would apply to lots of
schools and not get in anywhere. I had not yet begun to imagine
my life in New York. I didn't know what it would feel like to mine
my own life for stories about my body and forget that the sky was
anything more than a blue strip between tall buildings.

Onstage, I did an arabesque, lifting a leg behind me and turning it out and keeping one hip down, toe pointed and beveled, legs
straight and back pulled up up up. It is a beautiful line for my body.
In ballet, the perfect woman's body is built like a top. If you're built
like a top you can spin like one too. I'm not built like a top, but I
work with what I have. Although I could never spin, I held that
high arc of the arabesque for two counts, three, four. In arabesque
I balanced, waiting for a man to rush over and take me in his arms,
lift me above his head, and spin me until front looks like back and
back like front.

After four counts passed I saw the others dancing. I was supposed to have joined them. I was supposed to be stepping forward
with them from one world to the next, swatting the air from my
way, and going to the ocean. I was supposed to have been scanning
the horizon with them as though looking for faces in a crowd.

But then, I could feel myself dancing, one foot moving before
the other, doing exactly what I was supposed to do without even
realizing it. The spell was broken, but I noticed something else
was not right. There was a looseness around my foot, around my
ankles—my pointe shoe had come untied—and I worried fran-
tically the others would trip while trying to keep doing the choreography. There I was onstage at the beach in my green 1920s
swimsuit, the style from the year my grandmother was born, part
of some man's dream. I wished I could press pause on this moment

to retie my pointe shoe ribbons, and keep my lips from sticking to my teeth in my stage smile. I didn't want this to happen during my last performance. I didn't yet understand that it would make a good story later.

To keep your ribbons from coming untied there are a few things you can do. You can sew them on, but I had to switch shoes three times during that performance. You can spray them with hairspray or glue them with eyelash glue, but I didn't do this. I was going to grad school when this performance was over, and it was as though I was testing how low the stakes could be.

Somewhere miles below me my shoe had begun to come off in my final ballet performance of my life, and the ribbons were trailing behind me as I walked to the water, the edge of the stage, to cool off after a long dance. The ribbons flapped loosely behind me with each step.

I quickly calculated what steps were still to come, whether I should run backstage and either rip the shoe off or retie it, but I knew all we were doing was walking towards the ocean, which was the cliff of the stage, and then looking out at it, into the dark cavern of audience, which was the horizon, the seam of land and air. My shoe didn't matter.

After these last steps, as the stage lights went dark, I ran backstage to get rid of my shoe before the final bow, consumed with thoughts about how I would get in trouble later, and the director would fine my paycheck, and the pictures and reviews would be ruined because I couldn't even tie a shoe. Blood had wept through my tights, so I put my shoe back on and stuffed the ribbons under my foot, still untied. I thought of my friends and family laughing sympathetically afterwards, trying to make me feel better about the untied ribbon, and how I wouldn't laugh. "I don't even want to talk about it," I would say. I had broken the spell of the ballet and the green swimsuit and of Ravel. I have never seen such a thing as an audience member, a pointe shoe ribbon coming untied, so unprofessional, so careless. I thought of the ballet director being disappointed in me, how I would try not to cry. The ballet had been written with a happy ending. I wish there was such certainty in life as well.

I bowed, alongside the man in the blue swimsuit, to a black wall with applause coming from it. In the morning the papers would say one of the ballets that night highlighted "the weightlessness and delicate footwork of four dancers, particularly the sylphlike Ellen O'Connell." They didn't mention my shoe. Looking back, it seems like the perfect final performance, with a glowing review and a blunder that would never matter again.

In the wings I saw a woman in black pants and thick gray hair that curls over her shoulders. I could hear her saying, "Ellen will never do it again. I think she's probably being hard enough on herself right now." I walked towards her, relieved it was all over and also acutely sad. As I walked off stage, it occurred to me I wouldn't do this again—walk offstage after crowding it with my own body's movement. And I have kept that promise. When I walked into the wings, it felt like walking towards the rest of my life, which lay somewhere offstage, waiting for me to claim it.

I could not have asked for a better metaphor for the last time I was a ballerina, the last time I pretended my body could cooperate with the demands I placed on it. I had ignored the smaller, softer signals my body had sent me that I was making it do what it could not, that I could never force it into an entirely new shape. I should have read that trailing pointe shoe ribbon as a sign too, but back then I was focused on trying to control every muscle in my body and every ribbon and snap and zipper that held it together.

Ballet privileged how my body looked at the expense of how it felt. At no point in any ballet class I ever took was there a chance to revoke or rethink my implicit consent to teachers, choreographers, and partners who must, for the aesthetics of ballet, touch women's bodies to perfect positions or movement—either directly or, by encouraging us to dance even when our bodies felt very, very wrong. Now, years removed from daily classes, it strikes me that it took leaving this world for me to untangle my injury from the movements that caused it, and instead see it as the result of something much deeper. I had to forgive myself for learning the lessons all women learn of ignoring our own pain, of accepting it as normal.

I would have never believed that I'd leave ballet behind and become a writer, that my compulsion for self-expression would change channels but not intensity. It would have seemed inconceivable to me that obsessions can change, by constraint or by chance. There were other, less drastic options than forcing my body into a mold it would never fit. I knew my plans had changed, that I wanted to hold that graduate school acceptance letter in my own hands, that I wanted to move to New York, where Isadora Duncan and Martha Graham both went when California seemed too remote. It was the end of more than just a performance, and more than just a night. I knew that somewhere behind me, in a dark theater, a young girl left the stage in one shoe, walking past a grand piano and a musician in a tuxedo never to return. I was already forcing myself from her outlines, leaving her trailing me like the ghost of a past life.

"A dancer dies twice," Martha Graham said. "Once when they stop dancing, and this first death is the more painful." As I danced onstage for the last time that night, I was dying my first death, a death that had taken years since my fateful back injury. When

Wendy Whelan retired from her career at the New York City Ballet, she said, "I imagine it like death, where you look at it and you're afraid of it. And then you actually experience it and there's no pain." The pain had passed long ago. "It's actually blissful," though, she said. "And it's out of your hands." Perhaps that's why, that night, I floated. In my memory, it was, up until that point, the best I'd ever danced. I loved ballet again while I danced to Ravel—loved it for the power and grace I felt in my body, and for knowing it no longer had a hold on me.

PART II

10

My first semester of graduate school, I saw a woman lying dead on the pavement somewhere on Sixth Avenue, somewhere between Broome and Vandam. A police officer squatted over her, playing with his phone while he waited for backup. People passed by as though it was not at all strange or shocking that she was lying there, reminding us of our own mortality, right in the midst of a Saturday afternoon. When I caught sight of her, she was on my left-hand side, and I looked away so quickly that I have always doubted my own memory. Her lying there, the pavement under her cold and as gray as the sky above her.

It felt like an undignified ending to have New Yorkers step around you, barely glancing down. At least that's how I remember it as a twenty-two-year-old away from home. Seeing a person freshly gone filled me with a dread so profound it hung over me for days once the shock had worn off, and I never felt the same way about Soho again. It is a clever trick of the mind that I forgot where this was, exactly, because I never avoided a street corner so much as I did a memory of a ghost, conjured even now each time I smell a pretzel cart or see a lovely Christmas display in a store window.

I had been on my way to a Spanish grocery store to buy some smoked paprika for my mother, who told me she had started using it when she cooked. Somehow, I thought if I could find it and send it to her, I could bridge the gap between us, between the discoveries we were making without each other. So I kept walking to the store, determined to keep living.

I imagined the final moments of the woman in an office building stories above—the smooth plastic of a wooden-looking desk beneath her feet before she jumped. She could have spread her palms over the panes of glass, which trapped the December air outside the room. She would have stood for just a moment, looking out over the city of New York, full of people looking askance at each other as they passed through the veins of boulevards. Maybe she stood on her desk as though the figurehead on a great ship, with all the sound turned down to a peaceful lull. Papers stacked on her desk, her potted plant watered. This all began years before, perhaps with an isolated incident, or perhaps with a slow-spreading disease that began in her aching temples and worked its way down to the arches of her feet. So she did the only thing she could think of. She found the latch of the window and opened it. Her hands were not shaking; that would have passed long before.

And just as easily as a dropped napkin or a scattered dandelion in a wind gust, the woman jumped. Or at least that is what I imagine happened in order to give myself a story to cling onto rather than a lifeless body to puzzle over.

⚬⚬⚬

"Have you ever seen a dead body?" a boy had asked me earlier that year, as we sat together in a late-night restaurant in Santa Barbara. We sat close together in a wooden booth, facing one another, knees touching under the table. He was someone I knew from college—the one who had watched me in my final performance.

"My grandparents," I had said. Although having been raised Catholic, I had been to plenty of wakes, and had once served mass for a child who had died, the tiny coffin dwarfed by the flower arrangements on either side of it.

"You've never seen one on the street?" He had picked me up from a ballet rehearsal because he liked sitting in the theater watching me for the final five minutes and then waiting for me to change into the clothes of a pedestrian. From far away he memorized the shape of my legs, and then at dinner he touched them up close.

"No." I replied. He always tried to point out the ways I was young, naïve, although I was never sure what he was trying to prove.

"I don't think there is anyone who grows up in South America who has not seen a dead body on the street. In Spanish we call it *besando el pavimento*. Kissing the pavement," he said. I remember thinking how unlikely it would be to stumble on a dead body.

Kissing the pavement is a romantic phrase that belies its malignancy. Kissing the pavement was a poetic way to say that a body had stopped working as it was designed to, that it had stopped working at all.

❧

When the woman on the pavement landed, her body tried to keep right on crashing through the sidewalk. Although the skin on the woman's face was just skin, there was something horribly distorted now, a certain and soundless shatter of her bone structure until it was not a face, but one continuous line of eyes and nose and mouth, all vertically arranged. The way her face was turned it looked like she had her ear pressed to the sidewalk to hear what was beneath. One arm was flung behind her body. I don't think I could have invented that image.

New York and its ability to look away from life's most shocking images was teaching me exactly what I could adjust to. I learned to keep warm in cold weather and to live frugally in a city too expensive for graduate students. A few days a week I caught the Harlem train from Grand Central Station and ended up in Bronxville, where I walked up a steep and often icy hill to Sarah Lawrence College. In old dark rooms we sat around tables discussing literature—the classics and our own—and because I was so homesick, nearly everything made me cry. After classes, when I took the train home, I took long walks to get to know Manhattan too—miles and miles—and ended up finding something new each time.

Though I had dedicated years to the MFA, it was difficult to know where to enter my own writing. I wrote about boys I'd liked who hadn't liked me back, or fights I'd had with my parents, or a trip my family took on a boat when my brother was my greatest companion, but none of it felt compelling or urgent in any satisfying way. I thought by focusing on smaller-scale pursuits—finding the paprika, a small park to read in, a cup of tea better than I made at home—they would give shape to my homesickness, and the dreadful embarrassment I felt at being so adrift.

I called my parents in California and told them what I had seen. The next week, I told my thesis advisor at Sarah Lawrence, a woman named Jo Ann, who said, "If I saw a dead woman on the street, that would be a metaphor I'd return to over and over." That week, I wrote my first essay about ballet: about my big fall and injured back and my own anchored body on my parents' floor, my own vulnerable body in recline, which the dead woman must have stirred in me.

"You could write a whole book about ballet," Jo Ann told me in my next meeting with her. Those words ignited something for me, gave permission I wish I didn't need, validated something I didn't realize I'd doubted all along. By telling me I had something to write about, Jo Ann was asking me to articulate exactly how much I'd already overcome.

❦

People are composed of so many parts. I learned in ballet that a human foot alone has twenty-six bones, and when even one of them breaks, we say the foot is broken. The entire body, mostly filled with water and roughly 75 percent more bones than the foot, sometimes has one small part of it that fails. Sometimes when the part that fails is an organ, we say the body is dead, when really the rest of it could have kept on working for decades. When the woman landed from the ledge she left, her body smashed and smashed until there was not a part of it that could have gone on. And yet. Only some of her bones might have splintered, only some of her organs may have been taken by death.

❦

Around that time, I began going to therapy in a Union Square office with a woman named Camilla, who asked me to tell her a different story than I'd been telling myself for years. Therapy worked nicely with writing—both asked me to consider representation of interactions, objects, and people. With Camilla's guidance, I considered my interior life, and for the first time worked to create a new narrative not formed by the choreography I'd danced, nor the ballet culture I'd grown up in. Week after week, sitting on that couch,

I talked about my terror of a snake I'd seen when I was nineteen. When Camilla asked me to describe what it was like to see the dead woman on the pavement, I spent only a few minutes telling her about it, then quickly rerouted my story to my fear of seeing a snake.

"When I ask you to talk about seeing a dead body, why do you talk about the snake?" Camilla asked me.

I had no idea how to answer that question. The snake was a red-striped king snake that moved past my right foot one spring day as I sat on a cliff over the ocean. It appeared just after my final big ballet injury, and at the exact same moment I registered the writhing snake, I was pulling away from the kiss of a boyfriend who, that day or maybe the next, held me down on his bed and forced me to have sex with him. When I talked to Camilla I said it was not terrible, that we'd had a misunderstanding—I'd said "no" but only once, or maybe I'd been laughing when I said it, or he could tell that even though I'd said "no" I was curious. But losing my virginity this way had made me lie there, still and weeping, as he finished on top of me. "You said no," she said, as though it was that simple.

I couldn't explain why I was fixated on the snake and not what happened after. I thought of that snake before I went to bed at night, and throughout the day when my mind was quiet, it seemed to slither across my brain, creating full-body tremors. My friend Annie once told me that after she had known me for a week, she knew two things about me: that I used to be a ballet dancer, and that I was terrified of snakes in a way that seemed to organize and structure my entire life. How ballet had led me to this consuming phobia was the next great project of my life, one that would take me over a decade to tackle.

A block after I passed the woman, I sat down on the curb next to a mailbox and let myself cry. But by then, I wanted to poke her, to step hard on her with my whole weight, to punish her for having jumped where I could see her, to show her my contempt for her being dead. By being dead she reminded me that death is not separate from us, but it is closing in around us at every moment. I wanted to study her but from a great distance, perhaps in the pages of a book. There is no armor better than understanding the particular set of circumstances surrounding death and its laws. I wanted to hold this death down under my thumb so it wasn't loose and hanging over the intersection, being ignored in this way until I noticed it. I wanted to keep it where I could see it so it didn't sneak up on me again.

I went online and searched desperately through police reports to see if I could find an answer to who the woman kissing the pavement was and what had happened to her, but found nothing that answered my real question—why some bodies die while I kept on living. I looked though obituaries that first night, knowing no one would have had time to write one yet. I thought maybe by knowing who she was, I would understand something about what it meant to stay safe, upright, and alive.

Writing about the dead woman I'd passed gave me the voice to say what I wanted to say the way ballet had in my earlier life. It allowed me to make a muse of anyone, including myself. It also allowed me to work through the sight of a dead woman, pinned to the cold sidewalk that Saturday. I thought my desire for expression was made manifest in ballet, but I was only now learning to tell my own stories.

With each new essay I gave Jo Ann, she told me to keep digging, to keep polishing the small memories that surfaced and string them together and try to make sense of how they were all connected. But there is so much the reader can't see when we choose a metaphoric image too, so much we keep offstage.

I thought I could make a metaphor out of death, but I did not realize that I could use it to foreshadow too. That was still tucked years in the future, like the pages of a book.

Both Jo Ann, my professor, and Camilla, my first therapist, asked me to author the symbols of my own life's events. But it would take more living and more writing before I could articulate the symbolism of the snake, before I fully understood its power over me, before I released it. That my phobia of snakes was, in fact, as big a lesson as ballet. Still, I wrote and wrote about ballet and the pain I put myself in until I had a book's worth of my own stories, and although I've rewritten each one countless times, I was using my body's response, the same one that makes me sway whenever I hear the neat 4:4 time of Chopin's Études. But ballet was only the first half of my story.

I had already used one chance to get back up from the floor, and might not have another.

11

Just as the late spring arrived in New York, the trees erupting
and the air growing sticky, I graduated and moved as quick as I
could back to the dry heat of California's central coast. My first
week back, I went to my friend Hannah's parents' house to swim.
They lived in a beautiful stone ranch in the Santa Monica Mountains, where Hannah grew up listening to the animal sounds outside her windows at night. All my friends from college were there,
swimming topless in the pool under the warmth of the midday sky.
I was sun-drunk and needed a glass of water.

Walking up the stone steps from the pool to the house, I heard a
loud buzzing sound, like a wind-up toy. My eye followed the sound
to a rattlesnake, draped like a shadow up the staircase I was ascend-
ing. Just like the first snake I had fixated on all through my time
in New York, this rattler was only a few feet from me when I saw
it. Escaping from that rattlesnake felt as critical as it felt impossible. I knew I could never escape—even when I was safely in the
house, that snake would be waiting outside for me, buzzing its loud
electrical warning. A firestorm went off in my brain, and I forgot
who or where I was as I tried to make my way back—if you'd asked
me right then to conjure my mother's face I couldn't have done it.
Even now, writing this, the snake ripples like a fault line through
my mind.

Hannah said she heard me and ran to find me. "I knew only one thing would make you scream like that," she told me years later.

The next thing I remember after seeing the rattlesnake is my feet in a bucket of ice water and my head against Hannah's stomach. "Breathe," she was telling me, over and over. A group of friends stood around me, clucking sympathetically. Hannah stroked my hair as I wordlessly sobbed against her. The edges of my vision blurred like television static.

"Our gardener flung it into the bushes," Hannah was telling me, her voice coming in and going out again. "I grew up in this house and have never seen a rattlesnake this close to it," she said, holding my body against hers. "I think your fear attracts them."

I don't remember the rest of the day—how I got to the car or drove home to Santa Barbara, where I was living with my parents. But I sensed the world had tilted on its axis. After spending those years in New York discussing the idea of a snake, it hadn't occurred to me I would see one the week I returned to California. In some ways, it gave my fear legs and let it run. The experience made me mistrust my own home, knowing how much danger might find me. There was nowhere I felt safe, not even my own body.

⁂

After I saw the snake, I stopped hiking, walking through grass, watching movies unless someone could verify there were no snakes in them. My family wasn't allowed to say the word "snake," so we spelled it out using the radio alphabet: Sierra November Alpha Kilo Echo, "Sierra Novembers" for short. My friends called them "land eels." It was easy to pretend my fear of snakes didn't affect my life as much as it did when I avoided any possibility of going anywhere I might see one.

I didn't let anyone kiss me for five years, certain I would dissolve or cry or seize up and forget how to use my lips. Kissing felt unimaginable the longer I went without doing it—one kiss might indicate someone wanted to keep kissing me, which meant I would have to remember, during a quiet moment, what had happened to me, and how I had not been able to escape it.

The night I met Justin, I was making a Ouija board on the coffee table next to a pregnant woman. It was a dry August evening in California, and my friends had thrown a theme party where everyone dressed as a witch or a wizard even though it was months before Halloween. The year before, I had gotten a teaching job at the university where I had gone as an undergraduate—one class each quarter at first, but gradually building up to what amounted to half of a life. I'd left New York and moved home. Cut off from the world that seemed to matter, I was feeling unprepared in many ways for a steady job discussing serious literature. It felt like erasure to go back to the place where all the childhood selves I'd shed waited for me like thirsty ghosts, so I stayed out late with new friends and tried to manufacture a life I could write about. Parties like this set me on edge, all those drunk boys lunging, the loud music everyone else knew the words to, the conversation in a corner where I had to shout in someone's ear or turn my own ear to his mouth. It was a constant performance that left me feeling tired. When I saw Justin, I had an eyeliner lightning bolt on my cheek and he wore a pointy hat. Both of us had someone else's hand touching our shoulder in a gesture of forced intimacy.

Our friend's pregnant wife also seemed overwhelmed. I cut the letters for the Ouija board from bright construction paper beside her, taping all the way to T before Justin leaned over and said, "We shouldn't conjure spirits next to an unborn baby." I didn't believe in black magic, and neither did he. In fact, thinking back on it now, it seems out of character for him to worry about it, but sometimes our childhood beliefs cling to us like moths.

Long before I fell in love, I danced it. In ballets, the falling in love is instant, requiring no more than a look. When I danced the part of Clara in *The Nutcracker*, I never thought about my prince— instead I thought about the rotation of my legs in a grand jeté and making the audience fall in love with me. It taught me a lot about being loved, but next to nothing about loving.

I see us now, his close-cropped haircut, my focus as I smoothed my skirt over my hips, and imagined myself on a dark stage with a single pinprick of light. The memory is pure heat, but that night I didn't recognize him as anyone other than a stranger. The Ouija didn't work—we couldn't get good answers without asking good questions—and in the amber-filled evening someone cast a spell on me. "The next person to look at you will marry you." Justin was by then in the other room unclogging a sink, but he came in the room where I sat, still wearing rubber gloves, and said, "Nobody look at her!" Then he looked at me for a beat, turned, and walked back to the dish-strewn kitchen. I could barely meet his gaze, let alone jump into it. It felt too much like a spotlight.

Later that night, after we'd circled each other a few times and drunk to the center of our glasses, Justin told me he was moving home to New Hampshire in a month. I asked him if he'd miss the landscape he gardened where the air smelled like dry leaves and jasmine and salty skin. And although we had never really talked before, I wondered what it would be like if we were characters in a ballet who let ourselves be overtaken by each other. But by then I hadn't danced in five years.

What's so great about New Hampshire? I asked him.

His brother was having a baby and he wanted to be near his family, he said.

I told him I'd done my fifth-grade state report on New Hampshire but had never been. I'd written a poem on the cover of this report, its final line "The best thing about New Hampshire is it snows."

"I'd never seen snow when I wrote that," I said.

"There's plenty of it back home. Do you still write?" he asked me.

"Sometimes," I said. I thought of myself as more of a dancer than a writer, even though I didn't dance anymore and I wrote all the time. The new self-identity felt presumptuous, like wearing an expensive dress I was borrowing from a friend—I was afraid to claim and dirty it. I'd had over two decades to think of myself as a dancer, and my back injury had done more than just reshape my days. It had changed the way I thought of my worth in the world.

This story, like all stories, is concentric, each line we repeat an escape from its previous meaning. Years later, Justin reminded me of my fifth-grade snow poem while we were trapped inside during a blizzard—the best thing about New Hampshire is, it snows. It was funny in a moment of cabin fever, and felt like a relationship thundershirt, a callback to who we once were to each other. But that night at the witches and wizards party, as we stood next to each other as we played "light as a feather, stiff as a board" with a group of people, I felt the heat from Justin, and radiated my own back. Bodies fall in love long before minds catch up.

⁕

In Europe, when people clap for a performance that truly moves them, they clap in unison, an unheard, unfiltered rhythm which drums itself into the space between each person, so that in sound, at least, they are bound. I've heard it happen only a few times; each time it catches me by surprise and I can't help but wish that all performances were this way. They clap for the man who saved the woman from her own fate, and for the grace with which she was saved. I'm giddy with the thought that I know how so many people feel at once. It's one of the moments in which my child-heart is so full that the only way that seems to stop its overflow is to join in.

I have missed ballet every day since, and yet am disturbed by what, exactly, I'm missing. Some of what ballet gave to me, and some of the things I miss, have been satisfied both by falling in love with Justin and by writing down what it felt like to train for two decades to be one person, and then realize being that person would break me.

⚜

A story without an ending is just as hard to talk about as pain without a name, because I can't decide what the climax is—a bigger one might be coming if I'm patient.

Before Justin moved back to his hometown, he kissed me on the couch of the apartment he was staying in. Once he kissed me, I didn't want him to stop, but I was terrified I'd sob into his mouth, or we'd get to a point where I couldn't back out. He kept stopping to look at me, as though reading my eyes in the dark. I worried he'd think I was fragile, weird, skittish. I thought I was all those things. But instead, he took his cues from me, which made me, gradually, relax, glad I'd waited until I'd found someone who checked in with how I was feeling. The next morning when I woke up, I had a stomachache so acute I went to Urgent Care, where they told me I was fine.

That fall, he came over after my dog ate the blinds in my apartment to put up new ones. I made him an olive frittata one weekend morning and he ate it, although six months later he told me he hated eggs and olives. At his goodbye party, he pulled me into the garage and kissed me hard and long once again, our first secret.

In October, when he finally drove back across the country with his childhood best friend, I baked them chocolate chip cookies for their road trip. The first night Justin was gone he sent me a picture of the night sky in Utah, where they camped. I wondered whether he wished I were there with him. With our bodies removed from each other—our physical presence a hole through which we slipped—we told each other stories.

He told me about the time he fell out of a tree and broke his arm.

I told him that my dog runs away, and each time I accept he is gone for good, he comes back.

Justin described his snowman, stories tall, that ended up on the cover of a magazine. I described the experience of waiting in line for a falafel in Paris, and how the sign out front had a quote from Lenny Kravitz declaring it the best falafel in the world. I could not imagine eating one with Justin someday, although I would have liked to; the materiality of him eating, chewing, swallowing was abstract to me. He was a lover without a body, a voice on a phone, words on a screen, a memory. With each new text or phone call the record of my memory updated, adding in a new piece of information that never quite added up to a complete person.

I sent him an extra copy of *The Things They Carried*, which I was teaching at the university that quarter—thinking of how it was in my hands, and would next be in his. I wondered what he would recognize of Lieutenant Jimmy Cross, the soldier with the picture of Martha, a girl he barely knows. Inventing someone to shape our needs is a dangerous game—books taught me what ballet did not.

I found some comfort in the letters of other lovers who had been separated and still, in the end, had come back together. Perhaps like all readers, I looked to books to better understand my own human heart. In July 1944, the composer John Cage wrote a love letter to Merce Cunningham, one of Martha Graham's company dancers, and later a choreographer in his own right. Cage wrote, "i really need not be with you for me or for you, because there was facility in inventing your presence and knowing that just then you were merely not visible or not audible." Both men composed—one for instruments, the other for the instrument of the body. I imagine being both artist and muse—a luxury rarely afforded to women— and wanted to be a student of other people's obsessions with ballet, with bodies just out of reach. Like Jimmy Cross inventing Martha, like John Cage inventing Merce Cunningham, I invented Justin, and then tried to fall in love with the person I'd made up. The pain of long distance drove me to write my way towards some illumination, but writing a body into existence gave me no brightness, just more hunger, more pain. My mind was not up to the task.

By the time I finally flew across the country on my spring break to visit Justin, a near stranger by then, I had almost forgotten his face. He picked me up at the airport in Boston with a pair of purple wool socks he'd bought me, because I'd told him I once asked Santa, as a child, for pink socks and purple gloves—he'd gotten the combination wrong, but of course that didn't matter. When we saw each other, I was more focused on how I looked than about how he did, but even non-dancers must fall prey to this same trap. I watched his face as he first saw me. I felt my own body quickening, and his too.

As he hugged me hello, he said my hair was longer, and I was smaller than he remembered. Maybe he'd invented a version of me too, one he was now replacing with my physical body. He was a surprise to me too. I kept my hand on his shoulder as we drove back to New Hampshire, just touching the very fact of him. I walked around his home as though it were a museum.

The next morning, we found an American flag buried in the sand at the beach near his home and went back twice to dig it out. I was fascinated by every detail of the material person—the sheets he slept in, the toothpaste he used, the way he asked for the check in a restaurant. When I went home to California a week later, I could almost see our way to a happy ending. All we had to do was commit to memory while we were together, and imagine each other when there was a country between us. This was how I solved feeling seen when my body was removed from physical proximity.

When we visited each other over the next several months, Justin and I kissed in airports, at bus terminals, in restaurants. We held hands as we walked down nice blocks in the cities we lived in and chose which house we would want. I liked the houses painted in unexpected colors, he liked the ones with big yards so he could grow us a garden. I missed him even when I was with him. On each coast, we had our favorite houses picked out, but we didn't know the people we would be if we lived in any of them.

Once, he drove me to another state to see a movie I wanted to see. It was about a hotel and all the strange people who live in it, and we held hands until we needed them to eat popcorn, and then we touched knees in the dark. I looked over at his face, washed in flickering movie light, and tried to remember the feel of him next to me. He was not one for grand gestures, for proving a point or keeping me from an invisible tug towards some terrible world.

He would not make me a muse, a dancer in a green bathing suit flitting around a dream on a seashore. He forced me to be more fully human than I understood at the time. Justin was loyal, quiet, humane, hilarious. "My love for you is a given," he told me, once, when I asked why he didn't bring me flowers or declare his feelings. He was a scientist, his mind working in knowns and absolutes. He was the kind of person who didn't mind having a sandwich every day for lunch, even when I wanted chicken tikka one day and quiche the next.

I felt like John Cage, begging Justin to remember me although he never gave me a reason to think he wouldn't. Later the same summer John Cage wrote to Merce Cunningham, he asked him to "please be lonesome enough to come back in not too distant time." The request was to remove distance, to replace it with a body. Letters provide the best biographies—what's the use in knowing who went where and when? Letters can tell us instead who said what, who didn't say what. What was in the mind, what the heart pressed up against. It was hard to believe a thing had happened if I did not tell it to Justin, and did not hear his reply. My phone, too, became precious, its own quick means of hearing from him, of getting a picture of where he was, what he was seeing, what he noticed about it. I was too used to the idea of getting a man to drink me in with his eyes. Falling in love with Justin required me to write.

I wrote letters just so he would save them. "Your letters i just plain love: they bring you so close that at any moment i expect the door will open and you will see me camouflaged in enigmatic home, built on shoes you made," Cage wrote to Cunningham. The written-down words collapsed the difference between the body and the mind again and again, leaving a trace where a body left none. Words on a screen were not as good as a thing held my hands, pressed shut with warm lips and sent to me, to feel the thrill of a stuck-shut letter, dried from the spit trail of a tongue I could only imagine.

In the end, it was hard to fall in love over thousands of miles, when what we really wanted was a pair of those warm lips to kiss goodnight. Sure, we visited each other and had late-night phone calls. But we tried not to ask so much of someone we couldn't lean over and touch.

We stopped and started again. The distance made our story a series of coming together and pulling apart. It was not tidy—its edges bulged, it was both more and less romantic, time elongated. Love was not as I imagined it, both more painful and more lovely. I stopped trying to solve the distance, or to bridge it. We tried breaking up, to see if that made sense. I had no role to step into, whose ending was already written, no character in a ballet or a book to imitate. Balanchine once said, "There are no mothers-in-law in ballet." There is so much that cannot be said with ballet, where there are rules for how to move and how to dance. Long distance relationships were like Balanchine's mother-in-law, a real problem without a representation to study.

This all felt like a new phase in my life, the one in which I was becoming a writer, and figuring out how to process the years I had devoted to dancing so that they didn't feel wasted, or silly. Justin and I tried to solve each other, when really it is ourselves we were puzzling out. Was I becoming a writer, and what did that mean? Could I write about this life-in-process? We asked each other concrete questions: What are you doing this weekend? How was your Christmas?—but they were not the ones I wanted to ask: Is this an opening or closing? Coming or going? Ready to join me, or let me join you? The familiar feeling of not being seen was hard to solve. Asking him to see me from three thousand miles away felt too demanding.

"I can't focus on my life here if I'm always thinking about you, across the country," he told me on the phone one night.

"I understand," I told him, pretending I did.

⚜

"Falling," said Merce Cunningham in a 1970 interview, "is one of the ways of moving." It is a virtuoso feat to stand on one broken foot in an arabesque at the end of a solo when you're sixteen, I think. It is also a feat to fall and to stand back up and try to dance again.

"Within the body's limitations, I wanted to be able to accept all the possibilities," Cunningham said. Limitations in movement—both geographical and kinesthetic—allowed for other ways of using our bodies to see each other. Knowing me after I was a dancer feels incomplete, but so does knowing me only as a dancer. When one identity was removed as a possibility, I had to rely on the imperfection of the other. There are limitations to seeing and being seen because we are performing our roles so imperfectly, without virtuoso feats, with only the quiet ways our two legs carry us towards one another. There is no perfect way to fall in love, and it will always be different from what we imagine. We compromise, we try so hard, and care so deeply.

The night Justin first leaned over and kissed me, the month before he moved, I didn't know love was something to decide on. It seemed as fleeting and expressive as a dance, and as permanent, and far-reaching, as something that was worth writing down. Ballet had so many gatekeepers, I'd never had the power to decide the course of my life by, say, following love across the country, or by seeing my fear of snakes with tenderness and compassion. Meeting Justin, and recognizing my phobia's roots in my loss of power, opened up a new avenue towards healing, and for the first time, I held the keys.

Bodies might change shape, but not ardency. I have loved like that twice in my life, which makes me lucky. The first time I was nineteen, dancing in a rehearsal studio without knowing I would ever stop. The second time I was in my twenties, cutting out construction paper letters for a Ouija board that couldn't tell us the future. Both times I was unaware of the story I was moving through. I didn't know Justin would become more familiar to me than ballet. I just knew that it was a night like any other, only, like all moments we remember as our life's climaxes, it was the start of something else that would take me years to name.

12

There are layers to every story we tell, and to all the performances we give.

For six months, Justin and I stopped talking. I tried to replace him with dancing, just as I tried to replace my love for ballet with him. I woke early one Saturday in summer, when the sky had fanned high over me, and said, I think I'll go to a dance class today. It was the first time I had thought that in about five years, so I remember it distinctly and unequivocally—by then I was writing almost as much as I used to dance. I felt heartbroken my love affair with Justin had ended partly because we no longer lived close to each other, partly because he was afraid he would disappoint me, mostly because we were slipping through each other's fingers. He wasn't grasping tightly enough to hold on to anything but handfuls of me.

Many years had passed since I had last danced, but I still had a recurring dream where I would go to the ballet as a spectator, but when a dancer is injured, be called on to step in for her. I dug through the old leotards in my closet and picked a green one. I hoped I still had some ballet shoes without holes in the toes, but at first all I could find were pointe shoes, dirt-stained satin wearing thin around their edges, perhaps the pair I had worn eight years before when I fell and broke my back. In that drawer full of old dance clothes, I found some canvas shoes and walked out of my bedroom into my parents' house. I had returned there as my love affair ended to feel less alone. Though it had been many years, the sight of me in a leotard was so familiar my mother didn't even look twice.

The sun was drumming long fingers against the ballet studio when I arrived, and I walked in and told the teacher I had been a dancer. Ballet only, I said, but I couldn't do ballet casually now; it would be like dating someone I was once married to. Hour by hour, in that first class back, I looked at myself in the mirror on the studio wall and thought: what a miracle. My muscles shivered with memory. I pieced myself back together, bone by bone.

⚜

I had only taken one modern class before, during my first quarter of college as a dance major. It was hard for me to learn combinations that didn't have specific words and names that referred to the direction of my body, as ballet did. In ballet, I learned choreography by knowing where onstage I was, what direction I faced, and repeating the words of each step I did until the movement became automatic. But in modern, learning to perform movements with directions like "contract," "spiral," "fling," meant next to nothing to me. They made me feel even more directionless.

Maybe to reclaim some sense of my own direction as an adult, I wanted to dance the way Martha Graham had, to feel the wildness, to feel the ground. Martha Graham changed dancing the way Van Gogh changed painting or Faulkner changed novels. She had seen what worked and what was outdated and invented something entirely new that lasted long after she had died. Dance could give something new to me now. Dance would no longer control me.

Dancing like Martha Graham meant I did not have to worry that it wasn't the right way.

In writing, there is a primary document to return to, a novel, a play, a single word. But in dancing, like in love, the movement is ephemeral, tied to a certain body, existing, as one writer put it, only so long as that body survives, and remembers what it has learned to pass on to someone else. I can point to the pain I feel when I dance and someone can lay his strong hands over the ache and almost feel it, if he is the kind of person who can be still and silent for a moment, if he has the kind of hands that can unlock me from the cage of my own body. The two art forms have their similarities too: both dancing and writing make my rib cage toss with breath, and, in some moments, can cleanse me, from the bones out. Love does that too, when it is good.

I read about Martha Graham a lot during my break from Justin. She choreographed 180 dances; only 40 of them survive. But she left more behind than that. She gave us women dancing barefoot, off pointe, so that they didn't need to be guided and supported by men, and were not hobbled by the shoes they had to wear. She gave us the idea of dancing from your sex organs; she said her dances had always existed, that she had been chosen to receive the "lonely terrifying gifts" of invoking them. Certainly if they existed before her, they exist still, after her death, if we could remember them with only our bodies.

I loved Martha in a way I don't love ballet, because she choreographed parts for angry women, an emotion more real and less sylph-like, and because she invented a style of dance when she didn't like the movement that existed. She was the first dancer I loved solely from reading about her. Her body and movement were completely imaginary to me. I had not yet seen her on film.

She began her choreography not with an idea of a character, like a story ballet, but with movement. She said, "I did not want it to be beautiful or fluid. I wanted it to be fraught with inner meaning, with excitement and surge." When I discovered there was a style of dance, that summer, that required me to think not of how I looked but of how I felt, that distinction replaced, without my knowing it, an unexamined childhood obsession with getting my body to look right in the mirror, an obsession so complete it threatened to possess me. To drive me to see myself as the heroine of any story I told, Justin as my inevitable prince. It made no room for his reluctance. Learning how Martha Graham danced felt, for the first time in my life, like something didn't have to devour me in order to earn a place in my thoughts.

As I wrote, I had dreams of being on stage again, behind a curtain, and hearing the audience become quiet as the orchestra began a slow and joyful opening. Because I'd just begun modern dance, which allowed me to feel my legs' power and my arms' beauty again, I thought of Martha Graham as a muse. She went to high school in Santa Barbara, just as I had, and I wanted desperately to find her home—it was as though I thought this would heal me further. But for the life of me, I could not find where Martha Graham had lived in California, where, in her words, she had gotten her wildness.

I spent hours looking on the computer for her house, asked other dancers in town, but it didn't lead me to her old home. I thought that maybe, at her front door, I would find some origin story of myself. Instead, I had to learn about her from the deep squats we did each day in class with our hands pointing to the ground, our heads thrown back, our eyes like an untamed horse. I didn't want to share her spiritual suffering, but I wanted to share her movement, which, in certain lights, felt like I'd never experienced her first death until an hour into the class, when the searing pain reminded me I was already living my second life.

All I could find about Martha Graham's home, at first, was that she and her sister, Mary, ran on the bluffs over the Pacific Ocean, where I had spent my childhood and recent years, and had written about all the years in between. Eventually, my mother and I went to the historical museum, where the librarian found the old records. The Grahams lived on the corner of Valerio and Garden, two blocks from where I grew up. I like to think Martha and I passed each other's houses often, overlapping in space but not time, the opposite of how I first got to know Justin, with whom I overlapped in time but not space. All of this was a comfort, clicking into place as I wrote my way through it.

The version of myself that lived in a dance studio had long ago vanished, but the version I found was older and less wounded. This version could use my body to take me new places and do new things simply by leaving ballet, and all it represented, behind me. When I walked into that dance studio with a broken heart, I already knew the ways dancing couldn't save me. I knew that I could not yet escape from my phobia, but I had already escaped from the belief patterns of my childhood. This time, escape wasn't what I was looking for. I was looking for all the girls I'd been, and all the ways I'd outgrown them. But so many of them were still in me: the soft hush of them stretching before a class, tying their shoes and tucking their laces, trying, but never quite being able to reliably execute a triple pirouette except by accident, and never by turning counter-clockwise. All of that was still in me, as was the knowledge that it mattered less how my body looked in the mirror and more how I could use it to express the deep memories of how to dance and how to feel joy. And there I was, the writer who could record all these lost selves.

I could smell the Pacific Ocean, its deep blue yawn, from the front doors of the studio that summer, as well as the motor oil smell of the hardware store next door. The day, outside the windows, heated up, beat on. In the studio, there was a row of women in front of me, and a row of women behind me. There are all the people we are at once, when we allow them to find their homes inside of us. I did the same movements Martha did, the same contractions and sweeps of limb, but each body moves differently. Fear still limited the freedom of my movement, keeping me on the well-worn paths rather than letting me go wild. I wasn't yet dancing perfectly—not with all of myself, and not as truthfully as I could have.

⁂

After my second modern class, I relinquished my small-hearted belief that modern dance was for failed ballet dancers. The teacher told me to come to advanced classes, even though I had never done modern dance before. After all, I had trained so long in ballet all over the country, and I was healing and remembering what it felt like before my back had broken, before my heart had. I walked in to the class feeling dainty and scared, but sure of my turn out and pointed feet. Once we started moving, the women, those dedicated warriors, pounded their legs, stomped their feet, smiled as they dove into the floor.

"Beautiful dancing today," the teacher whispered to me after class. It was a small compliment I carried with me during the day. In modern dance, my skin woke up, my feet didn't bleed as they had in pointe shoes, I forgot what time it was. I was aware of how it felt to move more than I thought about how I looked doing it.

Writing about dancing through my heartbreak was as natural, perhaps, as simply dancing through it, and one revealed the other.

Since there are layers to each story we tell, each time we tell one
we decide which layers to peel away, and which to let remain closed
over the tight bud inside.

There were a few days when I would cry so hard I'd hiccup,
but what person doesn't? I thought of the spring, when Justin visited me and told me he would bring me some succulents before
he moved across the country. He met my family, we drove up and
down the coast and into the mountains, we drank too much wine
and stayed out too late. We kissed at every red light. When he got
back home he was distant for the first time, not returning my calls
until days later, leaving me to guess what I had said or not said,
what I had been or not been.

That was what had made me come back home, only home
wasn't California or a person. It was a dance studio, which, like a
church, looks roughly the same everywhere you go. I found myself
inside.

✦

When I last visited Justin in New Hampshire, I woke up and heard
that the house had a heartbeat. I listened to it for a while; it was a
beat that could have been coming from either one of us. His pulse
was in his neck and I watched it, as I had plenty of times before, but
forgot to tell him about it when he woke up. I felt it drumming into
the creases of my clavicles. Somewhere outside in the forest, the
deer were stirring from their beds, stomped down and fresh with
the indentations of their warm and fragile bodies.

"Do you hear that sound?" I asked him. Sleep left him like a
flock of sparrows, wild with birdsong.

"The frogs?" he asked.

"No, that pulsing," I said. "Listen. Can you hear it?"

For some moments he was quiet, and I wondered if he had fallen back asleep.

"I'm not sure," he said finally, which seemed almost impossible because it was so loud in my ears. "Maybe it's the hot water heater, or the fan," he said. I wished he had not told me the logic behind what I heard, but then this was one of the ways I was learning we were different: he liked to know how things worked, and I preferred just to believe they were caused by magic. Because I feared this gap between us, which spread wide like an unhinged jaw, I hugged him tighter.

Trying to describe the sound I heard, if only to myself, brought me closer to describing what we are. Life can so easily be lived unconsciously, and suddenly I realized how lonely I had been, and it felt like a homecoming to see Justin beside me, buckling under the weight of easy sleep. That, without willing them to, our hearts beat steadily, never forgetting that they were small machines that hummed beneath the sounds of living.

He pulled me into the heat of himself where I curved to rest and was still. But I was awake by then, my own heart beating louder because of whatever I heard in the house, so I got up, went downstairs to put on the teakettle, and opened the back door. A brown bird, perhaps a female cardinal, flew in immediately and sat on the window ledge, its tail unfurled in the shade.

"Oh," I said. "You're in the house." And with that the cardinal began the wild, desperate dance of birds trapped inside, slamming its small-boned rib cage under its thin layer of feathers, over and over against the glass. Outside the path stretched like a wide artery down to the field, which was waiting to be planted.

I could not get the window open, and the bird would not wait for me to try. I called upstairs.

"There's a bird trapped inside!"

"Right now?" Justin asked. He appeared in the room then, rubbing his eyes, and told the bird it was safe, which made it pause in its thrashings for a few seconds.

"In literature that's a bad omen," I said, after we got the bird safely out the back door. I almost said, it means there's about to be a death, but I couldn't think of more than one single book, out of the thousands I had read, in which a bird was trapped in the house and someone had died. It was a distant bell, something remembered but never questioned, a motion of the brain and an automatic thought.

"Let's hope not," Justin said absently, as he walked to the front door and stood, backlit, as though chosen by the sun. As the morning claimed the house, I sat on the couch and opened a book.

"You pick up a book whenever you sit down like it's muscle memory," Justin said to me, wistfully, as though he wished he did this too.

A few years ago, I had picked up the habit of visiting writers' houses when I went somewhere new, which I had said during a late-night phone call from one coast to the other. "Drive an hour in any direction and you'll find a writer's home," a friend had said to me before I left home to visit New England. I felt this promise coursing through me, something familiar and important in a way I could not have articulated, an ancient heart within my own. I wanted to see what writers saw when they looked out into their own fields and then transformed that view into something non-material. During one visit, Justin had surprised me by taking me to Robert Frost's farm on the way back from an overnight visit to Vermont. He had bought me syrupy hot chocolate and we sat on Frost's frozen stoop and drank it. The house had been boarded for winter, but Justin had wanted me to see the sign that said Frost lived there as a writer, teacher, and farmer. I was a writer and teacher, and Justin was a farmer.

When I had realized where Justin was taking me, once we passed a sign for Frost's farm, I had felt something shudder through me like a howling wind caught in winter's throat. I had wanted to kiss his eyes and the backs of his hands, his shoulders, his muscles, his joy.

One night in New Hampshire, on one of my visits, we picked our way through the darkening woods and I felt a new story forming, one I thought sometime in the future I would tell Justin, should we live to see it together, to see if it matched my version.

On our walk through his woods we made tracks in the mud rather than the snow and the ferns brushed against our legs. In his newly plowed field something caught my eye and made my stomach drop.

"What's that?" I asked, already running away from it, knowing the answer.

Justin stopped and looked at it. "Oh, that's a dead snake," he said. He knew I was afraid of them, but had never seen my phobia in action. I was petrified he wouldn't stick around if he saw how I reacted, but I could barely breathe.

I clutched my arms around myself and tried to catch my breath. "I'm more afraid of those than I am of dying," I said. To me, seeing a snake was like already being dead.

Justin took my hand, stepping around the dead snake in the grass.

"You're safe with me," he told me. "I'll move it later so you don't have to see it again." He pointed out the moss, the animal tracks, the forest floor, and each time I responded I was responding to that tiny dead snake, rather than to what was happening in front of me. I wanted to explain why I was scared of them, what had happened when I was nineteen and had seen one when I felt unsafe in so many other ways, but I didn't. I wasn't ready to release that fear, perhaps, to let it out in to the wild where I couldn't keep an eye on it.

Instead, Justin helped me pick a fern to press, which I did when we got back to his home, in his college science book, and I forgot it and flew back to California without it, and to this day it is still in this book, somewhere in the bookcase in our spare bedroom, although I have never checked for it. He says he knows which book it is, which gives me comfort that it will be there when I need it, or else it would surprise one of us one day as we go through old things.

⁓⁓⁓

Six months passed and we didn't talk. I went to visit two friends in Boston, close to Justin's home, and we got snowed in. Justin drove through the blizzard when I told him where I was. It took him hours, and he left after work, arriving sometime after midnight. The whole time I waited I kept thinking *he will turn around. He will not think I am worth this struggle.*

He showed up so late, telling me he'd taken the next day off work, and I recognized that through these small gestures, he was more dependable than the lovers I grew up watching onstage or reading about in books. It was during that blizzard we sat in the house with my friends' family and barely ventured outside, that we decided we would call the shots in our own story. Annie still takes credit for our marriage, for inviting me to Boston and for Justin visiting and for the snow that socked us all in.

A family is a collection of people we don't choose, until we do. When he asked me to marry him three years later on a walk in Maine, after so much stopping and starting, he said: "Can we be a family?" He asked me this despite my phobia, despite my back pain, as though our family could make room for all our imperfections.

As a woman who grew up dancing in story ballets—the kinds of ballets with plots and characters popular in the 19th century—I am addicted to the idea that love can cure anything, that it climaxes in a declaration, a vow, a wedding. The moment we decided, in the midst of a snowstorm, to make this long-distance love work might have been a zenith. So might the moment I moved to New Hampshire, finally becoming the pursuer, tired of waiting for love to befall me, for Justin to solve it when the answer was in my hands too. So might our wedding have been, once we returned to California two years later, or all the years after when we came home to each other every night. Love, I learned, was not a story ballet, but something I could find in Justin's home state or mine, as we sang to our dog, made each other lunch in the morning, took road trips. Love's zeniths are moments created by facing each other and being kind.

13

I finally moved to New Hampshire to be with Justin. When I arrived, with two suitcases and my dog, and waited for my car to be shipped across the country, none of it seemed real. I was desperately worried I'd never find a job or a tribe, and almost physically ill missing my mother and my best friends, even though I'd gained Justin. I hadn't felt so lonely and unmoored since I lost ballet.

That first month or two in New Hampshire, there were too many hours in the day. To fill my time, I napped, I looked for new teaching or writing jobs, I called my mother and cried, certain that I had made a huge mistake by moving there. Without having to lesson plan for my university classes, my days lost their structure. Well-meaning friends told me I finally had time to write, but I was gripping too tightly to the edge, and if I loosened my grip to write, I was certain I'd fall. Instead of writing, I drove down to Boston to interview for jobs I didn't get.

On the porch of Justin's cabin, I read for hours, turning, as I had after my injury, and in all the days since, to books for comfort. I almost choked with recognition for Ifemelu in *Americanah*, whose move to America and desire to live and write felt like a whisper of recognition. I read *The Woman Upstairs* by Claire Messud and felt too keenly the ways she wanted to be recognized, and the

ways she trusted others to do this work for her too much. I reread
Mrs. Dalloway, which had given me assurance when I'd read it years
before. They were friends to me when I didn't have many. Once
again, I pieced myself back together. Survival was, by then, muscle
memory.

During the evenings I waited for Justin to get home and try to
pretend I didn't check the clock every twenty minutes all afternoon.
Some days he was the only person I talked to. When he was late
coming home I cried, panicked he was with people who demanded
less of him than I did. He wouldn't save me, because neither of us
realized I was waiting for this, but he kept coming home and listening to me cry and stroking my hair. It would have been easier if he
demanded something of me, but he wouldn't, and this was what
carried us through.

Flight is a noun from the Old English *flyht*, Saxon *fluht*, Norse
flótte. A declarative word, something impossible for human mechan-
ics, but intriguing to our ambitious hearts. Birds take flight, but
people can only follow in dreams or metaphors.

Justin's backyard was full of wild turkeys, flocks of them that
visited nearly every day. They could not fly far, but it was a perfect yard to fly over, since it was long and straight. They hopped or
flapped to a tree, confined to one place, clumsy and alien. I heard
them call to each other, watched them walk slowly around, saw the
appealing ugliness of the skin of their necks. Whenever I saw them
I thought of Sylvia Plath, who remembered turkey necks and turkey gizzards the first time she ever saw a naked man. It depressed
her. The days built themselves, vast and empty. I watched those
turkeys, clumped together in the field, chasing the sunlight from
the bruise of early morning. They, like all poultry, adapted to living
on the ground, so when they sensed danger, they could not take

flight the way a hawk would. That they were trapped resonated with me so deeply I thought they must recognize me too.

Before I moved, I asked Justin what he most looked forward to when we were in the same place. "I can't wait for us to eat the same things, so we'll be made of the same things," he told me. My old life leaned in close, whispered goodnight, and left me alone. Each night I tried to cook elaborate meals. We were made of vegetables from his parents' garden, hand-minced garlic, ten-ingredient sauces. We fell asleep in his cabin, where birds sometimes got trapped inside, afloat in an ocean without shores in sight. Once we turned off the lights, I felt tears run into my ears. Only one of us had a life there, and both of us were trying to live it. We were made of the same material, but who was stitching it?

In Hebrew the word *brh* means a pre-emptive flight. It is related to the word for "to become homeless," which is what you become once you take flight. Homeless, trapped in a great field, trapped in a traffic circle. Once we take flight, the air around us is a new home, our place in it transitory, migratory, wild.

When I saw the turkeys in the yard, alone or in pairs, unable to take flight, I knew I was learning something about myself from them. I was learning to be fully self-reliant at the same time that I learned to be reliant on another person. I have never liked the idea of self-reliance, but I could not find my flock so far from home.

❦

Those first few months in New Hampshire, I took Eli, my dog, on long walks around the marsh. I listened to the whispering trees and focused on the smells and sensations, trying sometimes to imagine myself as a dog, as a tree, as something rooted or curious, not far from home and afraid of what I was doing. The roads were paved but the seam of them met the forest floor, a wild and moody tangle from which I steered well clear.

On our walk, Eli pounced, and a tiny garter snake winced beside me. Its yellow stripe, its small body sending me screaming into the road. I gagged on my own tears, running down the road, trying to rip the skin from my arms, unable to breathe, unable to escape the terror, or outrun it. A car pulled up to me—a convertible, possibly the only one I saw that summer in New England—and a woman leaned over.

"Are you okay?" she asked me. I must have looked like I was running for my life, being chased by an invisible predator, or else mentally ill, or on drugs, altered and at loose ends.

"I'm fine," I told her, through tears and sobs, "I'm fi-i-ine," the lonely and despondent wail of someone with no comfort and no shoulder to lean against. The woman took me at my word and drove away.

From the center of the road I realized my legs were leaden. Since I couldn't escape the snake with lead in my legs, I called Justin, only about 100 meters away, a distance that seemed impossible to breach. "I saw a snake," I told him. My throat was closed and my arms and legs were numb and untrustworthy. This was the first time he'd seen me directly after I saw a live snake, and it felt like a threshold from which we could never back away. He found me and drove me along the ocean, making me take deep breaths with him until I could speak again, patting the soft part of Eli's face— between his forehead and his eyes—like a worn blanket. Next to us, the calm sea inhaled and exhaled as rhythmically as we did.

The next day, my back was in a spasm, hung over from the fear I'd lodged in it. Fear caused pain caused fear caused pain. I could not pick or explain them apart until I tried. And for now, at least, I was not ready for that—I was too busy trying to make it to the next day to delve into darker territory.

❧

By the beginning of August, Justin's mom found me a part-time job at the school where she taught kids with learning disabilities to swim through the dark ocean of reading. It was a place to be each day, populated with people to talk to. I was used to teaching classes with twenty-five students, getting them to discuss, debate each other, fill the silences. But at this school, I was assigned to one student at a time during a teacher's medical leave, and when she returned, the school hired me to work intensively with a single student, whom I spent all day with.

She was Kayla, a student who could not see. She had never been able to see. She was funny and sensitive and was the only person in New Hampshire who I didn't feel like I was making small talk with. I had to learn braille quickly, so Justin and I studied every night and wrote each other notes in pencil and paper, drawing tiny dots, all of which were both letters and symbols for letters, both the thing and the emblem, like my spine, like my fall in ballet, like my second life. I brought home the brailler, which looked like a typewriter, and worked on catching up with Kayla.

Each morning I met Kayla at her school bus and walked her safely to the school building, where we started a complicated choreography of what she needed for each class. I was fascinated by the way Kayla moved. She did not have the same visual stimulation the seeing do, so she sniffed the air she passed through, smelling the warm bodies who had recently come in from the brisk fall, on the verge of turning. She knew people by their smell, by their footsteps, by their voices. She touched their hair, grabbed woolen handfuls of them. The other students let her. Outside, the trees undressed for winter.

I became self-conscious about my language in a way she was not. "Can I see that?" she asked me when I had something she wanted to hold. She redefined language and senses both. "Read" was something she did with her fingers. "See" involved smelling a piece of paper, holding it against her face, shaking it in front of her. "Look out" was something I said to her when she was about to crash her body against something, and she looked with her cane. When the other students praised her for doing things all able-bodied children could do, like pour water from one container into another, she told them, indignantly, "It's kind of insulting when you say that. I am eleven years old."

Kayla had a quiet friend, a kind girl who asked her one day in science class, what color she saw. "Is it just black through your eyes?" she asked.

"How would I know?" Kayla said. "I've never seen black." It could just as easily have been pink that she saw, the pink of eyelid, or the red of blood, or the white of bone.

Because we redefined the word "read," Kayla read much better than I did, though she was dyslexic. I was still trying to catch up with the letters and punctuation while she read contractions. And like dyslexic students who read with their eyes, Kayla got letters backwards and mixed up. A lower case *b* felt like a *p* to her.

Sometimes, to be funny or because they were uncomfortable, Kayla popped her prosthetic eyes out on the desk in front of her, lenses that covered her under-developed eyeballs like giant contacts with pupils and irises. They stared back up at me, and I knew I should be the one to rinse them and put them in her case, but I was frozen. I asked her if she wanted to learn to take care of her prosthetic eyes herself, and she said, "I'd be grossed out to touch someone else's eyeballs too." When she took them out in the bathroom, the most brilliant blue eyes stared up at us from the palm of her hand. They made a small clicking noise, and for a minute it was easy to forget which part of the body could really see. The prosthetic eyes made Kayla sit up straighter and open her eyes when she talked to people, keeping her from straining, but in her hand, they seemed redundant and absurd. She pinched them in or out, held them for a few seconds, feeling the weight of her eyes on the tips of her fingers. I once heard a boy tell another teacher that Kayla had beautiful eyes, but he didn't know they weren't real. Although her real eyes shrank because she never used them, the doctors wanted to keep them in case science ever advanced far enough that they could work. Kayla believed in this with a boundless, unmoored faith that took me back to a time when possibilities were all in the future, and all I had to do was secure those small hopes and worry them like stones in a pocket. "By the time I'm old enough to drive, there might be a car that will drive itself," she told me. I didn't say that I doubted driverless cars were headed to rural New Hampshire anytime soon, because the kindest thing we can do is to let people hope that everything will work out the way we imagine it, that all we have to do is meet each day, ready.

❦

While working with Kayla, I found, quite by accident, footage from the Perkins School for the Blind of Martha Graham. This led me in turn to a lovely story about her, one that fills me with recognition of something I've never experienced. When Martha Graham was a child, she often visited her father's empty doctor's office when he wasn't with patients. One such day, she climbed on a pile of books so she could see the top of her father's desk, where he was looking at a drop of water on a glass slide. When he asked her what she saw, she described it as "pure water." He slipped the slide under the lens of a microscope, and she peered once more through the lens. "But there are wriggles in it," she said in horror. Then, he gave her a lesson she recalled even as she dictated her memoir, *Blood Memory*, at age ninety-six. "Yes, it is impure," he said. "Just remember this all your life, Martha. You must look for the truth: good, bad, or unsettling.

"Movement," he taught her, "never lies."

"In a curious way, this was my first dance lesson," Graham dictated, "a gesture toward the truth. Each of us tells our own story even without speaking."

A few years earlier, and several states away, Helen Keller had her own revelation about water as she realized what was flowing over her hand from her family's pump matched the word her teacher, Annie Sullivan, was signing into her hand: w-a-t-e-r. "Somehow the mystery of language was revealed to me," she wrote in her own memoir, *The Story of My Life*. "That living word awakened my soul, gave it light, hope, joy, set it free," she wrote. "There were barriers still, it is true, but barriers that could in time be swept away."

For both women, water facilitated the web of connection between materiality, movement, and language, a revelation that led them, improbably, towards each other. When Keller was seventy-two years old, a friend introduced her to Graham, by then the doyenne of modern dance, who invited Keller regularly to her dance studios at 66 Fifth Avenue to observe. The two became fast friends. By the time Keller and Graham communicated with each other through Annie Sullivan's hands, both were already famous—Keller for untangling her blindness from her fate, Graham for believing that passion, not technique, was the pulse of dance. In her memoir, Graham says she was taken with Keller's "ability to perceive life through her own unique awareness," and Keller followed Graham's choreography by fixating on dancers' feet on the floor, which she felt in order to learn in what direction the dance was going. Graham, always on the lookout for ways in which people used their bodies to make meaning of the air around them, observed that Keller "could not see the dance but was able to allow its vibrations to leave the floor and enter her body."

The 1954 documentary *The Unconquered: Helen Keller in Her Story* shows the first time Keller went to a Graham company rehearsal. Graham is standing in a circle of dancers who run slowly around her to a beat we can't hear in the recording. On counts of three they land and pause, their arms waving overhead like branches in a breeze. Graham is wearing a floor-length dress and has her hair slicked into a chignon, dramatic, severe, and striking. Graham sees Keller and breaks through the circle of dancers to greet her friend, embracing her before leading her out of the camera's view, presumably to sit down or take off her coat. Periodically, Sullivan spells the action into Keller's hand.

Graham leads Keller over to a drummer with four drums in front of him, and Keller keeps her hands out, hovering in the air around the drums. She has taught herself to pay attention using the vibrations around her, and is still able to see and hear by following the directions of sound waves created by voices, bodies, and instruments. When Keller turns towards the camera, waving her hand through the air in front of her face, her face is awash in delight and wonder, for she feels what Graham's hands are not attuned to, what Graham cannot. Seeing Keller's unedited delight in this moment gives me such joy each time I watch her. It's a reminder that well into adulthood there are discoveries waiting for me to summon them. Keller's emotional stirrings are aspirational, although I'd like to aim for something of Graham too, who facilitated Keller's dance lesson and gave us our own.

Keller feels the scarf a male dancer holds, trailing on the floor. Although she has been to dance performances, says the narrator, "it is only in a rehearsal room, like this, she is able to discover with her hands, the line of body and limb that is the living pattern of the dance." Keller traces the man's leg as it développés. A développé is an unfolding motion, the foot peeling off the floor and tracing the shin to the knee, where it lifts to the front. Helen would have felt the hip moving, the knee, the leg bent to straight. She would have learned that in one movement the body undergoes a tautness and a languidness at the same moment. At that moment, she feels a woman who has joined the man with the scarf from her head to her toes, and the woman does a back bend away from him while Helen Keller traces the line of the woman's neck, feels the weight of her head in her hand, the curve of the sinew just under her skin.

Behind her, Graham keeps her arms on Keller's back like a dance partner, watching her, catching her. Keller is encircled with barefoot dancers in black unitards who step, step, arabesque, step, step, arabesque around her, typical of Graham's aesthetic. Keller directs them from the center-radius, her arms over her, joining in the dance, while Graham watches, dethroned from her role as director, explorer. How, asks Yeats, can we know the dancer from the dance? The answer to that seemed obvious to me until I watched Helen Keller learn how to dance as Martha Graham held her.

❧

According to Graham's memoir, in one of her visits to the dance studio, Helen Keller asked "What is jumping? I don't understand." Graham was touched by this question, so she asked Merce Cunningham, then one of her dancers, to stand at the barre.

"Merce, be very careful," she told him. "I'm putting Helen's hands on your body." She took Keller's hands and placed them on Merce's waist while he assumed first position. Around Keller and Merce at the rehearsal studio barre, people stood still and quiet, watching what was about to happen. Merce began jumping, and as he moved up and down, up and down, so did Keller. She would have felt his muscles spring and release very quickly, and the repetitive motion of her own hands over the machinations of his body. It is difficult to imagine going fifty years without knowing what it means to jump, and it strikes me as a shame most of us do not remember learning.

Merce kept jumping, and, Graham recalls, Keller's "expression changed from curiosity to one of joy. You could see the enthusiasm rise in her face as she threw her arms in the air." Over Merce's waist, Keller's fingers began to flutter as she learned what it means to jump, and how it is one way to dance. She had never, before this moment, experienced dance close up. When Merce stops jumping, Keller exclaims, "Oh, how wonderful! How like thought! How like the mind it is."

❧

Here is a metaphor: to be someone else's eyes. My job was to teach Kayla, and keep her safe, yet I could not see the world through her eyes. Instead, I had to listen to what might distract her, or let her know why something smelled a certain way. I had to tell her who was laughing, and why. I often didn't know the answers, but because I could see, I knew what I didn't know. I had the complete visual, but she had more clues.

The metaphor that existed between Kayla and me was plain and shining. Both of us had to find ways to exist within our limitations. I was far from all the people I had ever known, except for one person. Kayla was blind, and relied on one person. Both of us relied on the resources we had, most of which were internal and unconscious. Every day for us was heightened. We jumped off cliffs at least once an hour. I learned the same lesson over and over, from ballet and from Kayla and from my own body: you have to work with what you have. There is no other option. I'm glad we had each other, for a short time.

Because she was blind, Kayla had to stimulate herself different ways. She fiddled with things around her, like pencils or flash cards or anything she could touch. She shook and smelled things, listened to everyone speaking in the dark world around her. Kayla walked sensually down the hall of her elementary school because it felt good to rub her thighs together and feel her stomach and she couldn't see that no one else walked that way. I watched her hands caress her hips and her cheeks. Who was I to tell her to walk normally? If walking that way felt good, maybe I should have done it too.

In some ways that fall, I was the happiest I had ever been—when I looked at Justin, I saw him years from then, wearing Prufrock's trousers. But in some ways I was also the loneliest. In those early days on my own, every day felt like eating my own insides. Kayla taught me that being blind is not a disability so much as a different way of experiencing the world. We all have some different experience, I often thought as I watched her walk through the hallway. Being Kayla's eyes made the light go off, so I was forced to feel my way through without the senses I had always known but never noticed. Feeling my way through a new place with the use of my sight suddenly seemed like I could tap my way along, too. I could use what I had and sniff the air until I found my way, distrusting the ways I had learned to use my body when there were so many parts of it I'd ignored.

Each new day led somewhere I couldn't see from where I stood. I could not stop them, nor could anything. One day in December, just before I got a full-time job practically overnight, and left Kayla without having the chance to say goodbye, the whole school piled in the bus for a field trip. Kayla had been looking forward to swimming all day, but when we got to the giant complex, with an indoor soccer field inside a dome, a pool, basketball courts, and plenty of other rooms I never saw, Kayla asked someone to summon me to her in the bathroom. There she told me, "My underwear is all wet." I felt a responsibility so huge it nested inside my chest, spreading until it took up the space of an albatross in flight.

I told her what had happened, found a pad somewhere for her and put it in the dry bathing suit she'd brought. Because I could see that the back of her pants were stained, I told her to put her sweatshirt around her waist for the rest of the day. She couldn't swim, so instead she sat in the locker room and cried on my cell phone to her mother. "I just want to go swimming with my friends," she gulped into the phone. "Sometimes you have to be flexible," I heard her mother say. "I'm sorry you're upset. You're being very brave."

"Will you come get me?" Kayla asked. Her mouth grew smaller and more pained, like she was chewing broken glass, and of course, being a mother, Kayla's mother left work early and came to get her. She had Kayla's skis on top of her car, because the whole family was going skiing to make Kayla feel better about her confusing day, her body doing something new that she didn't understand. Her mother thanked me. I was relieved to let her take over from there, although in some ways, that was the first time I felt in control of anything since I'd moved. I knew what to do, what the options were, how to explain what had happened. There was wisdom in her body, and in mine too. The body signals, but our intellect filters.

When I met Kayla, I pressed my experience against hers like two wet leaves, imprinting what I knew on her. But the transfer was doubled. I took my findings with me, her particular way of seeing, her sadness when life was unfair. I took my sense of usefulness with me, marched right into my next job interview, and got the job.

I left Kayla. The full-time job offer came over the week of Christmas, and I started right after the new year, while Kayla was still skiing with her family. By then, I had given back the brailler, so I couldn't even write her a note to tell her goodbye, that she is funny and strong, sweet and sensitive. Instead, I imagined Kayla feeding herself on the sweetness of smells around her. I imagined her driving a car, her blue eyes following the sounds she hears.

❧

On the couch one evening when Justin was making me dinner, a small miracle happened. The days were getting longer, our windows were open to the sounds of peepers. I had just gotten home from a modern dance class across the river in Maine, and I was writing something that wasn't about ballet. Dancing made me feel less isolated from myself, as did writing. It wasn't surprising that one still unlocked the other. I danced until my back hurt and then drove home to ice it and write about how it used to feel to be a body onstage, eyes watching me in the dark.

I asked Justin what the climax was of my move to New Hampshire. In my mind, the move was made up of holes, of losses, of absences with wingspans so long I can barely patch them together in a shape that makes sense.

"Deciding that if we leave, we're leaving together," he told me.

We decided this after one of the eight weddings we attended one summer, my second summer in New Hampshire. Justin was driving. It was verdant, late summer and a song we listened to probably fifty times that summer was playing, or had just played, or was about to play. He said, "If we want to move, where would you want to go?" We made a list of the places we would like to be together. Leaving home for him had forced me to redefine home, to think about it in a way I'd never had to before. We carried these parallel lives alongside the lives we had lived, those we had lost, and those to come. We listed probably ten places we wanted to live, and ten places we didn't. We couldn't see what was beyond the edge of summer, but we knew it was beyond the brow of the next hill we passed.

Unlike Kayla, unlike Helen Keller, I may not remember the joy of learning to jump, but I'm determined to remember the safety of landing. This lesson, keeping myself safe from the threats I could predict, was getting closer. I could see its outlines as we packed our life and our dog in his car and drove west, through New York and the Ozarks, through the desert and the Rockies, and landed, home again, as we just were, as we will be in each new place. I thought about looking back to see the ground we'd covered, but it's second nature to look instead at where you're going.

14

❧

I land on the coastline in New Hampshire, and learn to call a strange new state home. I land in my own body, and start to see the membrane between me and the self that stopped eating. I land in love with someone else, and the great miracle of my life so far is that he loves me too. We get along so well, after a while, this turns into a fact, and is no longer something I distrust. Justin asked me, on our first New Year's Eve living in the same state, after we get home from a night out with his friends, "Can we move in together? Can we live together for the rest of our lives?" We move out of our individual apartments and find a home together—the bottom floor of an old house on a corner with great light in a bay window.

We have our first holidays together as a couple in New Hampshire, calling my family from far away as soon as they wake up, three hours behind us in Santa Barbara. I text Paige, the first time I've reached out to her in years because she had fallen so desperately into addiction—she'd lost all our family except her mother and mine. She texted me my first Easter in New Hampshire, wishing me a happy day, telling me she loved me. I never replied. To this day, this memory rattles me. Hers was the first death in a series that forced me, finally, to figure out which traumas I could control and which I couldn't, and reckon with my terrible phobia.

As chance would have it, I was home in California for my friend Hannah's wedding when Paige died. My mother received a phone call from my aunt that Paige had been found unresponsive by her roommate, was on life support at a hospital in Ventura. My parents jumped in the car and drove down the coast to be with my aunt as she sat beside Paige's hospital bed, waiting to see what would happen. It was clear immediately, my mother told me, that Paige would not live. Her brain function had stopped. My parent's knew their job was to give my aunt permission to take her own daughter off life support. That night, after hours of agony, with my mother beside her, my aunt did the hardest thing I can imagine—she asked the doctors to stop all intervention. After weathering Paige's addiction for over two decades, and never giving up on her daughter even when the rest of us did, she said goodbye. Paige died peacefully, with my mother and father and her own mother there with her. My mom sent the text in the middle of the night to our family. I let out a moan, thinking of my aunt's heart, how it would never heal. The pain of loss was physical. My mother and her sister each had a daughter who had been beloved by our close-knit family, and now only one of us was left. One had fallen prey to addiction after her ballet career ended, the other one had become a writer. I reached out for Justin in the dark, but his arms were already wrapped around me.

When I was a child, I sometimes could not tell the difference between my mom and her older sister from up close—they had the same memories, the same smell, the same tender way of loving me. But now they were separate—only one of them had a daughter.

❧

When Paige was in high school, she was cast as Aurora in her small town ballet company's production of *The Sleeping Beauty*. "You should have seen her feet," Ñaña told me years ago. "She lost all her toenails." This happened to me too in ballet, many times, but it was so common it was never the point of any story I told.

I imagine Paige, before I was born, dancing the Rose Adagio, one of the most demanding pieces of choreography in classical ballet, and cannot reconcile the body control necessary to dance this adagio with the person I knew.

Paige had a beautiful face, and like me, never minded the spotlight. I imagine her lithe and thin again, her legs exposed in pink tights, the Tchaikovsky music building in the auditorium, and wonder if she felt this dance was a climax of more than just the music. At her sixteenth birthday, Princess Aurora must choose from the four suitors her parents have brought her, and in choosing, she must dance with each of them, holding a series of balances. She starts by holding their hands until she is steady, and then she lets go, and balances unsupported, alone, relying on nothing but knowledge of her body's capacity. She must do the whole dance twice, holding eight balances total, sucking her stomach to her backbone, thinking "up, up, up," stretching out of her pointe shoe until there is nowhere to go but back down. The image that stays with me, long after Paige has died, is of that moment when she balances alone in this iconic adagio, when she has mastery of every sinewy muscle, when she knows that her body is hers alone. This is before she is controlled by any person, drug, or shame. For as long as she can balance her whole weight on one toe, her hand, her body, are suspended as if from a string.

"She is free," my aunt said over and over, after Paige died. Even in the seconds that she was free in the Rose Adagio, she was not free. She was under the gaze of an audience, the tyranny of the music's rhythm, each of her male partners demanding to continue the dance. But life might be only that: a chain of shadowy moments that flicker across the stage, a spotlight momentarily blinding us to any burden other than love, desire, violence, grief. If death feels anything like that freedom, the veil that lifts momentarily many times in our lives, Paige had merely shape-shifted to find shelter away from her body, away from this world.

There are truths particular to addicts whose families stop talking to them before their deaths: the hole left by their absence in their families fill up before they die. The Thanksgiving table was already empty, the phone numbers already deleted. With Paige's death, the distance between us has vanished, in fact, even when the guilt has not.

The Sleeping Beauty is a troubling ballet for its female protagonist, even by ballet standards. Princess Aurora's fate is sealed when she is still a baby, and no action of her own can change the course of her life. Even a dancer who holds the balances of the Rose Adagio perfectly cannot alter the course of the narrative: no amount of technical perfection matters to Aurora's life—the satisfaction of this momentary suspension of time and gravity is a moment, vanishing without any trace but the memory of what a body can do. As Aurora, Paige slept and was awakened by another person, whom it was fated she would love. Who was this boy? Did the memory of his pimply face bending over Paige to wake her die with Ñaña? When I imagine it, I replace the face with my nutcracker prince's from the year I was Clara, when I was the same age Paige was when she danced Aurora. Her character lost control the moment she took the hand of the final partner in the Rose Adagio, and in many ways, Paige did too.

There must have been a celebration for Paige after her performance, but when I ask my mother, she doesn't remember. "It all blends together with your ballet performances," she tells me. Was Paige told she was anything other than lovely, beautiful, words so connected to the mastery of her body, that she forgot she was anything other than a young ballerina? My aunt would have been proud of Paige, not for the last time. Later her expectations were different: the simple fact of Paige enduring.

Ballet class taught me the value of keeping stories secret. If we were injured, we knew to hide it. If we were hungry, we knew to ignore it. If we were not praised in rehearsal, we knew it was because there were so many of us, and there was nothing to be done except try harder, make fewer excuses, jump higher, turn faster, stretch longer. I stretched and starved my own young body until it broke, and when it broke I pretended it hadn't, and only then was I rewarded. Ballet taught me that. By denying what I felt, I could reach and reach until I almost touched another person's love.

Paige's story was not about her body, but it took place within her body. Her story was about her relationship with her mother, and mental illness, and how a whole adoring family cannot make up for a missing father. Many people can endure much worse, but Paige was prone to breaking.

❦

The last time I saw Paige was one night when Ñaña called me and asked me to come over.

"Paige is having an imaginary tea party with Alice in Wonderland in the closet, and I think she'll snap out of it in front of you," she said. She had an edge to her voice she usually hid from me. When I got there, Paige didn't snap out of it. Instead she asked me to brush her hair for the Oscars until my aunt called the police to find out what we should do. She was worried, and tired, and in no mood for nonsense. Paige locked herself in a room, and when three police officers got there she invited them to the back patio because she didn't want us listening. They talked for half an hour, and I sat with my aunt, holding her hand, in a way already replacing the daughter she had lost.

"I don't think she's a danger to herself or anyone else," one of the officers said when they came back inside. "She told us her family is angry with her because of something she did, but she didn't say what." So they left, and Paige went to sleep, and I fell in love and moved away and didn't reach out.

❧

The day after Paige died, I rose, showered, and got dressed to go to Ñaña. I could not bear to be away from her. When I saw her the next morning, she embraced me and told me, "This is not real. Don't worry. This is not real." She walked from room to room lowing in pain, her grief ripped from her, splitting her open with its jaggedness. When she was exhausted, she sat, and I went to her and dropped down, kneeling before her as though in worship. I will be other things as well, but I will always be a young woman, sitting in front of a newly daughterless woman, holding her face in my hands. My body was full of a painful emptiness. I cried with her, making the same noises she did so she knew she was not alone. I brought her water and when she could not lift it to her lips, I did it for her. "You are my baby girl now," she told me.

At one point she said she could still feel the weight of Paige as a baby in her arms. "I can actually feel it," she insisted, wild with bottomless sorrow. Her ferocity scared me; I could not stem its tides, nor keep it from entering her and taking up permanent residence. "I held her for hours in front of the window, and it was snowing, and I thought I had everything I needed. That baby and I felt like the whole world." She shrieked this, barely able to get the words out, and with one trembling hand stroked my head as though it were Paige's.

⁂

It was the day before Hannah's wedding, and Justin drove me to Hannah's parents' ranch, where I'd seen the rattlesnake all those years ago. Now we were helping her set up before the rehearsal dinner. During the car ride I alternated between crying out in shock each time I remembered Paige was dead and choking with panic remembering the snake as though it would be there waiting for me years later. Home did not feel safe, not when people you loved most could die or the thing that scared me most could appear suddenly in the landscape. Beside us, the ocean sparkled until we cut inland through the light green hills of spring.

"I'll check the ground for snakes," Justin told me as we got off the freeway, trying to alleviate my panic.

"No, it's silly," I told him through tears. "Just because I saw one there once it doesn't mean there will be one this time."

When we pulled into the driveway, I opened my door before Justin could get out, desperate to prove I was okay, that I could handle the day in front of us. And there, beside the car, was a small, white gopher snake, sunning itself.

My scream must have been blood-curdling. Hannah's mother came running out, and told me the snake was beautiful, and took a picture of it. Justin carried me inside to the kitchen, where my friends were gathered.

"We just saw a snake," he said.

"You've got to be shitting me," one of them said. "As soon as she gets here?"

My whole body seized, and I thought I would pass out. Hannah came and took my hand, and after a few gulps I told her I would be okay, and I could help her with an indoor job. She put me on flower duty, and Justin walked ahead of me every time I had to go outside to make sure the way was safe. That night as we fell asleep I sobbed against him, not sure how I could get through Paige's death and my own guilt, not sure how I could get through my phobia.

"How did I let it get this bad?" I asked him in the dark. He hugged me against him and told me I would be okay, but I didn't see how. I was too afraid of snakes to ask anyone to help me, convinced I had let it go on too long, and there was no way out. I didn't know how to dig myself out of this pit, or if I did, I didn't think I deserved help for a problem I'd pushed down for the last decade.

"We have to figure this thing out," he said. And I knew he was right. After some googling, I found a local therapist who specialized in phobias. His voice on the phone was calm and confident, and he reassured me that this was treatable. I made an appointment for a few months in the future, after our wedding, a promise that I would deal with it one day, but not right this second.

꧁❀꧂

Back in New Hampshire, it was still cold enough that I knew I wouldn't be in danger of seeing a snake for months. Swapping one coast for another felt like it would keep me safe in my phobia. "Coast" means margin on the land, meaning the edge of life and death. It is a distant cousin of the Slavonic word *kosti,* for bone. My bones felt fragile in the face of all that was holding me back, my dedication to calling my aunt each day, forgiving myself for ending my relationship with Paige, the fear of snakes that was with me every minute of every day.

Choosing a new home let me choose a new self to live in it. The self who lived in New Hampshire could avoid snakes, and could pretend it was just a regular fear, the kind other people have. But then I would see a garden hose or a coiled rope on a dock and start in terror. When you're that afraid, there is no avoiding the threat.

Justin applied to a job in California, in my hometown, and got it. Something about the circular shape of our meeting there, both of us leaving it, and it beckoning us back to live just before the wedding we were planning there, seemed like we had our own migratory pattern. When I watched Justin walk towards me in any town, in any light, I would know it is him from a distance, the way his knees bent and the way he approached me like someone I have known for a very long time. I had taken a risk and taught myself something in the process about my own ability to survive, away from my mother and home and friends and job. I could build a new life and step into it, but I could also leave it behind when I outgrew it, confident that someday soon, I'd stand at my kitchen sink in a new home, waiting for the kettle to boil, and think I have everything I need right now.

Going back to Santa Barbara meant coming home for me, but for Justin, it meant leaving his family and childhood friends behind once again, to return to the place he'd gone to college and grad school. I worried his family would think I'd dragged him away from them, even though he was the one who'd applied and gotten the job. But it was also exciting, in the month leading up to our wedding, to change the external circumstances of our lives so drastically when I felt an invisible shift in what was possible. I couldn't wait to live near my mother and aunt, near our yellow bungalow with light streaming through it every month of the year. Every part of my life that year felt like an internal homecoming, a return to where I had been but as a new person. Something in me felt settled, finally, as though I'd found the acceptance I spent my whole adolescence trying to claim.

15

One night shortly after we moved back to California, my aunt's husband called because she'd fallen and been on the floor for hours, but he couldn't get her up. "I think Justin and I could do it together," he said. Only when we got there they couldn't. I knelt on the floor holding her hand while Justin called the fire department, and three firefighters came and calmed us all down and spoke to her with dignity and concern, and she whispered to me she was humiliated. And I kissed her cheek and said, I know.

I wasn't sure whether I was witnessing the end of a life or whether I was nursing her back to another new one. Even though the answer was right there, it was easy to deny it. Justin and I had moved back to California just in time.

That summer, I read Ñaña her journal from college, with all of her poems and sayings she'd copied down from Kahlil Gibran and Rumi, from Emily Dickinson and Shakespeare. For a while I checked her face after each entry to watch her nod or open her eyes at me, and when she stopped doing that, I read them more quickly, desperate that I was running out of time to finish. We talked to her about the beginnings of things as well, of what had passed and what would come next.

Ñaña's breast cancer, which she'd fought a few years earlier, had come back in her bones and her brain, and she ignored it until it felled her, until her body seized control of her life's story. She didn't fully believe there would be a day after next—she was careful, suspicious, hedged her bets. Three months earlier, when her oncologist gave her a 70 percent chance of recovery, he told us all that cancer in the brain either originates there or migrates north from another of the body's planes. But my aunt defied the odds, her body overwhelmed with pain as it neared its end.

My mother was in charge that day as the doctor delivered the news, because my mother is good in a crisis—she has that kind of take-charge personality. She learned the rules from the hospice nurse and told them to us. She read the brochure about what to expect from death and told us what parts we should read, what we could skip because it had already happened. She delegated: my job was to offer food to people, which is always the easiest way to take care of a person's body, and to call my cousin Matt and tell him his mother was going to die today, and to please drive down quickly.

"Can you ask if they can hold off?" he asked me on the phone.

"There's no one to hold off," I told him. "She's going." He wanted the facts of dying: the color of urine, the temperature of skin, the pallor of eyes. I gave him them, because they seemed easier to understand than that death is our fate as soon as we are born, that as sure as we breathe and love and rage, we will die. Sometimes numbers and scientific processes are easier, less painful: one in eight women develops breast cancer. It's helpful to see the cracks we slip between.

Matt drove four hours to his mother's bedside, and sat with her. I saw her smile for the last time when she heard his voice. I called my

uncle, her younger brother, and said, "Now." He had been expecting the call, he said. He drove eight hours to hold her hand across
the river. I wished Paige could be here with her mother, but she was
on the other shore by then, maybe beckoning for her mother to join
her, maybe doing nothing at all. It had been a year and a half since
she died. It felt like a terrible, heavy honor to be with Ñaña now, to
watch, to shepherd, to comfort those who mourned with me.

Every once in a while, a hospice nurse came through the room
to remind us quietly that death was more than a metaphysical
experience. "Look for signs of pain," the nurse told us the morning
we realized it was her last day with us—lines of distress on her forehead, her body curling into a fist—"and tell her you're giving her
more morphine. She should look like a person dying in a movie,"
serene, hallowed, knowing. Even in death, we are performing.

My mother administered morphine every few hours, telling
her what she was doing, until Matt took over. Sometimes my aunt
could swallow it, sometimes she could not. This is part of dying,
although it is impossible to say what it feels like to have the living
interrupt you, calling you back to keep your pain at bay.

For several hours, each time she exhaled, she sighed, vocalizing
what sounded like surprise. Her face looked like at any moment
she could wake up and be delighted her family was sitting around
her. The night ahead of us stretched, unconquered. My whole body
hurt. And then each minute passed, taking its full time.

What was she hearing or remembering? Did she see people who
were already dead, or dream of the people she was leaving behind?
Was she seeing God? Paige? My grandparents? Was her brain simply shutting down under our watchful gazes?

In *Our Town*, Emily is already dead in Act III, and asks her
mother-in-law, who has been gone longer, "how can I *ever* forget

that life? It's all I had. It's all I know." And then "do any human beings ever realize life while they live it?—every, every minute?" But we don't, not even when we sit in the room with the dead, not even when we face it, when our body faces its own mortality by waiting for the death of another. Somehow, this cognitive dissonance is a luxury that allows us all to survive.

We can tell a lot about people's lives from how they die. While we sat around my aunt that Friday night, Matt played "Carrickfergus" for her, and I watched as he wiped a lone tear from his face. My beloved uncle thanked his dying older sister for helping him with his science homework in sixth grade, and for expecting that he could do it right, and for giving him Paige. My mother told my Ñaña stories about their childhood when their father was stationed in Ecuador, and the cast of characters only the two of them remembered, before their younger brother was old enough to play with them. I realized, looking at my mother, that once my aunt died, no one would be buffering my mother from old age and death, from decay and illness, and a feeling so big washed over me that I dared not give it a name.

My mother told us not to pepper my aunt with questions, which could agitate her, according to the nurse, and not to ask how she was or what she wanted. We made statements. I remembered our conversation a year and a half ago, in this very room, as she talked about the feeling of Paige as a newborn baby in her arms. The last words I heard my aunt say were to me: "my beautiful baby girl."

"What?" my dad asked her. I was panicked that he wasn't following the rules.

"She said 'beautiful baby girl,'" I told him, trying to save her in this one small way.

"That's what you are, Michelle," my father said to her. "You are a beautiful baby girl again now. Remember how you felt about Paige when she was born? Remember how she felt and looked in your arms? That's how God feels about you. You're a beautiful baby girl."

My father is a deeply reserved person, and I had never heard him speak like this.

Like all of us, he was looking at her body and seeing a story.

The hospice pamphlet says often, just before death, the person can become lucid, even after hours of sleeping, and can wake up and tell you something. We must not be fooled into thinking this is a sign of recovery, the pamphlet tells us. It is part of the journey of dying. Death does not come all at once, and it is difficult to spot unless we watch the rise and fall of each shallow breath, fearful that it will be her last, fearful it will not.

While she is still awake, I ask Ñaña if she'd like a spiritual person to come talk with her. We talked in euphemisms here. I could not bring myself to call things by their names—words she had never used before. She had never once admitted she was dying.

"A Franciscan from the mission?" I asked, thinking of the gold medal of St. Francis she wore on a thin gold chain around her neck. She nodded. A priest from my parents' parish arrived within a few hours to anoint her. This was the last time my aunt's eyes were open. While the priest read to her, rubbed oil on her forehead, he said, "God is very near you now, Michelle." She fell into a sleep for the last time—whatever was swelling inside her was no longer breaking her open. I could see the priest's words helped my uncle too, whose wife was dying, who remembered her as a college girl in 1967, when they listened to records together in the living room at his parents' house. They had both married and divorced since then, but came back together, and were married fifteen years, loving each other well. It is easy to tell stories of a life; what is difficult is telling stories of bodies: how they come together and break apart, what they house inside them, the automatic ways they know to carry out their days on earth. Bodies in this room do what seems impossible to minds: they die, they continue living.

After the priest left, my mother held her older sister's face in her hands and I watched tears trace from my mother's face to her sister's. "I have never known the world without you," she told her.

Ñaña's life had many endings in it, endings of marriages, religions, her daughter's life, and finally, her own life, which ended that day in August in her living room, where I sat touching her leg softly through a blanket. As the light fell across her lap and she uncurled from the pain of metastasized cancer into a morphine-sleep, her dachshund cried out for her.

In *When Breath Becomes Air,* Paul Kalanithi describes the state of the dying, the loss of vision, hearing, brain activity, like entering a dream state. Three-quarters of the dying dream they reunite with loved ones. At the end, different sections of the brain light up, and one of the last parts of the brain to shut down is the neocortex, responsible for vision, which is why people often see flashes of light dancing, an aurora borealis beating on the backs of their eyelids.

And then what?

"She goes back where she came from," my uncle told me. And when Ñaña inhaled, and exhaled for the last time, it was even more difficult to understand her experience. There were no dramatics— she didn't open her eyes or say anything. I wish I had asked Ñaña the right questions. I wish I had told her I was sorry we had all stopped talking to Paige. There was no other time to apologize. Death came quietly instead.

※

We went home late that night, got fitful sleep, and got a text from my uncle letting us know Ñaña was gone. I woke up crying, rose, showered, went back to the house. I repeated the same motions, with the same heavy feeling, as the day Paige died; only my aunt, lying in the bed where she had died, had changed positions. Her son slept next to her on the couch all night. My younger brother came over too.

The morning after she died we ate breakfast around her, spearing diced fruit, making toast, and any moment she looked as if she could awaken to join us. She was beautiful, her cheekbones high and light in the morning. She looked like my grandmother, and, startlingly, my own mother, although they did not look much alike when Ñaña was alive. The mood was lighter now that we were not afraid of the worst. It had already arrived. Eventually we made a phone call, and within one hour, three men in suits came to collect her.

"You may want to step outside as we put her on the gurney," one of the men told us. "The family can find it disturbing." Her son and her husband stayed, the rest of us went outside. Her best friend, who had driven four hours to see her, arrived as the men wheeled her out. She took a peek under the sheet outside, kissed my aunt's cheek, cried. A man with a dog threw the ball right next to my aunt, and the dog ran up and got it. We watched, horrified that he hadn't waited until after my aunt was in the hearse. My dad could not stop laughing, though, and later that day read us "Musée des Beaux Arts," by W. H. Auden, who describes "In Breughel's *Icarus*, for instance: how everything turns away Quite leisurely from the disaster." The death that was important to us did not mean dogs would stop playing, nor that their owners would stop delighting in the game.

The week my aunt died, my mother got her own chemotherapy port put in for a recent breast cancer diagnosis. Bodies don't get a break. Like my aunt's sorrows, originating in her left breast just over her heart, my mother's tumor was a parallel to her sister's; like Paige's love of her mother, my love for mine ran parallel.

When a person is wrenched free from her body, we mourn as though we invented it. Our bodies do what our minds cannot fathom, every day, in countless ways. The body outlives every other part of us—even our minds, which come into consciousness and lose it again before the heart stops.

16

The summer we moved back to California, the summer we cremated my aunt, Justin and I got married in Santa Barbara, where we'd first met. By the time my mother buttoned up the back of my wedding dress, she already had a tumor almost two centimeters wide growing in her left breast. She slipped Mita's gold bracelet on my wrist, identical to the one Ñaña had given her when Paige was first born, and walked me down the aisle with my father. I saw everyone I knew turn towards us in the church before I saw Justin, standing at the end, handsome and as close to crying as I'd ever seen him. My mother and father had not walked down the aisle of a church to organ music, the faces of loved ones beaming at them, since their own wedding. I asked both of them to walk with me because I didn't like the symbolism of my dad giving me away to my husband. Instead, my parents ushered me, together, from childhood to adulthood. I don't know how I could have made it all the way to the front of the church without both of them to hold me up.

Our wedding was on a rainy day in June, enough to mist a lifted face, unusual during a five-year California drought. On the outdoor lawn where we planned to have dinner, men milled around, trying to keep the chair cushions and tablecloths from becoming swampy; Justin went out to buy tarps that morning to cover it all up, like stage curtains. Neither of us worried the rains would not stop in time. It was all good luck, I thought. "It will be good for the pictures," my friend told me optimistically. The rain gave the earth a quick drink and then stopped in time for us to get married. I sat inside, telling myself, "Soon you will be married to Justin." I thought a lot about the afternoon in Maine, eight months earlier, when he had asked me to be his family, and thought how strange and wonderful we could choose to be joined like this, and how deliciously improbable we had decided, after all the to-ing and fro-ing, that we should.

I had always been the sort of person who thought of her wedding day, the girl who thought about growing up to be Clara, a dewdrop fairy, a bride. As I read magazines and looked through glossy pictures, I made a decision every day to keep eating, but I felt the familiar impulse to stop. Ballet had taught me the easiness of hunger, of shrinking for a performance. The wedding was a sort of show, after all, and I fought going on just one more crash diet during the last weeks of rehearsals. I had too much to lose now. Besides, the spotlight was not mine alone—it was mine to share, the people who watched me were there out of love, and I had nothing to prove to them about my own talent or ardency.

We got married in the church my mother's family attended, an old church seven blocks from my childhood home. Three of my best friends, my parents, and I got to the church at 4:58 p.m., right as the church wedding guild coordinator was starting to get nervous. When she asked Justin and his family what they should do as the wait for me dragged on, his father said, "I think we should wait for the bride." The wedding could not start without me there, and I remembered one other time in my life when they held the curtain for me, when I was fifteen, starring in *The Nutcracker*, just a block away from the church at the Arlington Theatre.

Justin writhed uncomfortably under the gazes of our loved ones, but I felt the familiar thrill of all eyes on me, waiting for me to step into the spotlight to join him. My heart swelled; the organ music built inside me the same way the orchestra music did during performances, just before I stepped onstage, the audience's anticipation fueling me, making me feel beautiful in my costume, my movements deliberate. I was afraid of ripping my antique dress and veil and so I took small steps. And like in ballet, we had rehearsed for months for one show only. Standing behind the heavy wooden church doors with my parents on either side of me, I felt the emptiness of my mind and the fullness of my body, just as I did standing in the wings for years, waiting to take my place.

After the wedding, its vows, its applause, its tears, Justin and I served the food to our guests in an historic mansion—he the salad and I the bread rolls—wearing aprons to keep our wedding clothes clean. We wanted to start our lives together by feeding our loved ones, thanking them for forming us and for traveling so far to witness our union. The aprons didn't end up mattering since I blew out the delicate lace armpits of my 140-year-old dress on the dance floor. It was practically made of spider webs, tailored to fit my body exactly, just like the tutus I wore in ballet. We danced to Dusty Springfield because Justin was the son of a preacher man. It felt like a beginning and an end, our delicate dreams of a life together, to be part of something sacred and homespun. In the following weeks and months, I missed looking forward to our wedding, but I loved remembering it.

My mother made a speech about how Justin was her son now too, and she would work hard to help our lives grow in love. My dad wished us a marriage as happy as his to my mother. We drank champagne under the cloud-blanketed stars.

The night of my wedding my mother wore a low-cut beaded evening gown, one that made her look as beautiful as she ever had, and with the faintest hint of cleavage in her dress, one she tugged at a few times, she was ever so slightly self-conscious, perhaps for the last time aware of her breasts as merely ornamental or a nuisance, as more than a ticking time bomb, more than the site of scars and radiation, more than a source of anxiety. By then, as she later told me, her breasts had done everything they needed to do. They had nursed my brother and me. There is a picture of her nursing me on St. Francis of Assisi's altar in Italy when I was four months old out of the same breast that would develop cancer. It is one of my favorite pictures of us. Today, I look more like her in that photo than I look like my baby self.

Our bodies that night were years apart, but closer than we could ever imagine. Six months after my wedding day, my father found the genetic report I'd left at their house alongside my mother's matching one, the twin anomalies making the distance between our bodies vanish. He said the similarity brought him to tears. But that was all still to come. Before all that, my mother marveled at all the details she had helped me choose for the wedding—the flowers she had arranged that morning with her friends, the bunting we had chosen together, the pictures of our parents' weddings next to our guestbook—that made it feel almost as much her wedding as mine. We walked around in awe of the night, as though in a museum we had curated, or a ballet we had choreographed.

⁂

I look like my mother, I move like her, I sound like her. Our gestures and inflections are similar, as are our jokes. She loves telling stories, reading, writing. She was my exact same age, down to the month, when she got married. What we couldn't have known on my own wedding day was that our bodies shared a genetic mutation. She had already developed the tumor, and I was only waiting to read the story written in my body.

My mother was always rough with my hair, maybe short on time or patience after having to pin it for ballet for the thousandth time, and I used to yell at her to be gentle. Until I learned to do it myself, she piled it on top of my head or at the nape of my neck in a tight fist, depending on the part. When I was Clara in *The Nutcracker*, she rolled it into curlers every night, so it would bounce for the next performance. Even after I was too old, I loved when my mother washed my hair, the hard way she scrubbed my scalp, and I would sheepishly ask her to do it every so often in the sink near the washing machine, my head bent forward, exposing the back of my neck.

After she had a partial mastectomy and her hair started falling out from the chemo, she asked me to come over one Sunday morning to shave her hair off. "It's too upsetting to watch it fall out," she said. My father charged his clippers, and I came over and draped a towel over her shoulders. She sat on the back patio where she used to give me haircuts as a child, only now it was me giving her the haircut, a reversal of our mother and daughter roles. The very action of shaving my mother's hair off was an ouroboros, a cycle of loss and growth, daughter becoming mother, a tail inside a mouth.

I shaved her head slowly, letting her know what I was finding beneath her hair—smooth skin and a perfectly shaped head. Her hair left a shadow on some parts of her skull that time would lighten up, but I knew I was the first person to see her scalp like this since her own mother, who might have lifted her baby hair and looked through to see the vulnerable pale skin.

Without her hair, she looked like a cancer patient, a role she could no longer turn on and off. Before I shaved her head, unless she told you, you wouldn't know you should be any kinder to her, or any more tender. But with her hair gone, she looked trapped inside her own circumstances, like a woman you want to help with her groceries or give your seat to on the bus.

❧

Cancer was a thing that happened to other people's mothers. This feeling never changed, even once it happened to my own mother— it was, and is, so improbable.

My mother found out she had breast cancer on the phone when she and I were at the hospital visiting her sister, who was, at that moment, dying of breast cancer. A mammogram had found the small tumor, her doctor tracked it for six months, and a biopsy confirmed what none of us could believe. My mom didn't want to cry in front of her sister because she always takes care of other people. That moment after learning her diagnosis was the first time she performed as a cancer patient. I don't know when she first cried, or if she did. When she found out she had to have chemo I tried not to cry in front of her because I didn't want her to have to comfort me, since this was happening to her, after all. That was the first time I performed as the daughter of a cancer patient. These performances were necessary kindnesses, in fact, a way to keep our emotional burdens from someone who has her own. There is always a body whose own end is more imminent, nearer the surface of eternity, than our own. We use our own to perform, and eventually to become, the kind of person we wish we were.

Thanks to the pink ribbon campaign, our culture's sensitivity to breast cancer destigmatizes breasts, though they are still banned from TV or the internet. They are sexualized even when used to feed a baby. We debate them, celebrate them, mourn the loss of them when they have a tumor inside. The lack of breasts bonds women to other survivors, as well as to those who have not survived, like my mom to her sister. Breast cancer also bonds those of us who live in cancer's long shadow, those who have a high likelihood of developing cancer thanks to our genes.

⚜

The day we got the news that my mother had a mutation in her BRCA1 gene blends with the day I found out the same thing. Both days, we were together, in the same room, alone with a nurse who apologized for telling us bad news, as though she were to blame. When my mother found out I felt as though I were hearing news about my own body. I had come from hers, after all. It was raining the day I found out, misty just like it was on my wedding day six months earlier.

The nurse explained the gene was a "misspelling." The sentence should have read "The big black dog sees the ball." Instead, my mother's and mine say, "Pig big ball black sees." Everyone's genes say something; I just read mine decades before the plot twist. I have a chance to change the plot, in fact. My mother does not have this same opportunity.

When the nurse said, "We found the exact same mutation in you," I felt a door inside myself close. But although my mother and I had a mistake in our bodies, our bodies themselves are not mistakes.

There is a range of statistics related to breast and ovarian cancers, and our risk is on a spectrum. When I read stories by other women who have this genetic mutation, they report only the higher end of these statistics. As a writer, I understand why saying "Nearly a 90 percent risk" is more powerful than the truth, which is that we are in a range of 57 to 87 percent risk. That truth is nuanced, complicated, less neat.

In reporting the high end's awful realities of our bodies, we say "nearly 90 percent," to justify the decisions we are being asked to make by the medical community, a performance to anyone we explain this to. Our bodies can turn on us unless we get our female reproductive organs removed: our ovaries, fallopian tubes, breast tissue, and according to some surgeons, our uteruses, which my mother eventually elected to do. It was hard for me to watch her make a choice about her own body I knew I didn't want to make for mine—to remember that although we are made of the same stuff, we are not the same. We both had to make a choice about having or putting off drastic surgeries that strip us of the very organs that can create life.

⚜

After so many years of back pain, I can finally get a doctor to take my body seriously, though not the way I want. The recommendations they give me to avoid cancer are pushy, statistical, dramatic. Starting at age thirty, I need to get breast exams every three months to check for tumors, including by mammograms, which radiate the very tissue that is prone to cancer—instead I pay out of pocket for ultrasounds. I should get my ovaries and fallopian tubes removed as soon as I'm finished having children, preferably by the age of thirty-five, to cut my risk of developing breast cancer in half. I can elect to either have my breast tissue removed as well, or to take my chances and continue being checked, which is what I immediately know I will do, despite the breast surgeons I see telling me this is foolish. Sometimes I look down at my own healthy body and think, will you betray me? When I hear the oral birth control, which will greatly reduce my risks of ovarian cancer, discussed as a luxury rather than a complete medical necessity, it feels like one more assault against my body, which by now has grown strong in the face of violence against it.

From my mother, I inherited the shape of my eyes, my love of storytelling, my small wrists and ankles, my long back, my sense of humor, my belief that after all is said and done, we will be fine. I inherited her chance of getting breast or ovarian cancer, and her resilience. I look at my mother's face in pictures from when she was my age and see my own.

In the weeks following this news about my mutation, it is easier for Justin and me to focus on the question of what to do about my ovaries than on questions about what makes life worth living. We go to a bar one night and talk about children's names, learning we don't like the same ones. Children become less hypothetical, more imminent, both of us afraid we will feel like we have missed out if we don't have them in our newly shortened window. The question of the purpose of the rest of my life is like background fog, too diffuse to pin down.

My choice is between having them before I was ready, or waiting and increasing my risk for cancer each year. I dream of traveling with Justin to Paris and Morocco, finishing this book, taking our time. We wish we could have children on our own terms, without feeling pressured by doctors.

The decisions I will make over the coming years wake me up in the morning, sneak up behind me during the day, overtake so many of the quiet conversations I have with Justin in the evenings. Everyone has advice for me, projections of the choices they've made over the years: the babies they have had or not had, the careers they've secured or given up on, the books they've written or regretted leaving unfinished. It surprises me that I knew what I wanted to do—wait and see, rather than remove my breasts—as soon as I first learned of this diagnosis, and how strong my resolve has remained. I give myself full permission to change my mind at any point.

If I have a daughter, there are lessons that I want her to learn sooner than I did. I want her to learn how to be friends with her body, how to be on the same side, how to tell it every day you love it, to thank it for what it does to move you through life. I hope not to pass on my genetic mutation. But if I do, I hope I also pass on all the things my mother taught me. I hope I love her as well as my mother loves me. And I hope I pass on the knowledge that we have to mother ourselves. Women learn to perform, to edit, to minister long before they learn to love themselves. One of the hardest lessons of womanhood is to treat ourselves the way we would treat others.

My mom finished chemo two days before my next birthday, and she got a short break before radiation. Her body shaped her identity as a sick person who tried hard to act healthy. Even when her cancer was in remission, it leaned against the doorframe, a shadowy phantom reminding us of the genetic predisposition that could welcome it back in the room at any time. My mother and I both take our bodies one day at a time.

The question of what to do with my life has become more urgent, although I try to break it down to the day: What would I do today if I knew I would get cancer? I would dance more. I would be so much easier on myself. I would keep working to overcome my terror of snakes so I can hike with my husband or walk barefoot with my friends, and so I don't pass that down to a child as well. I had already experienced my first death as a dancer. I would live my second life with all the compassion for myself that I couldn't spare before.

From a distance I see the space I take up and wish I could have allowed myself to take up all the space I have ever wanted. I would tell my future daughter to perform the roles she wants, and to shed the ones she doesn't. I would write my way into lasting beyond the final pages of this book, and write about my mother so that when her life feels threatened, I could preserve something of how much I love her.

I documented her illness, taking photos of her after each treatment, her head bald and covered in a hat, her fingernails swollen and discolored. I documented her recovery too, and it felt like writing a book, trying to pin down a body that resists permanence. It all felt automatic now—I was not just writing to make sense of my own healing, but because I was compelled to write, couldn't imagine a life without the precision of scenes and words, came back to it every day like ritualized prayer.

❦

What my body does without my bidding begins to fascinate me. The uterus and the heart have a lot in common: both swell and then shrink, carrying out a plan entirely their own that creates life by their very movement. The uterus is an organ that pulses blood through every vein, that we look to as the source of both life and love. For those of us with a uterus, a small drama plays out every month inside of us. It makes us attuned to the dramas outside us too. It means we can learn from others, from our mothers, that telling stories is a way to distance ourselves from the trauma we are bound to experience. We can mother our own bodies.

Like heirloom pearls, my ovaries are inherited from my mother, and like hers, will probably come out before they can develop cancer. If I remove my ovaries in the next four to nine years, my chance of developing breast cancer will be cut in half.

On our wedding night, Justin and I stayed in the hotel my mother thought was Martha Graham's home. In fact, her old home was across the street, but I was touched by the gesture; it shows how well my mom knows me. In a way, although it's less tidy to know we got the details wrong, my mother intended to give me the gift of my dance history, my body made grown up and new. After all, Martha Graham invented a kind of movement that didn't exist. All of life is seeing what is missing and using our own bodies to invent what isn't there.

Justin and I walked together to this house, across the street from Martha Graham's house, in our wedding clothes at midnight. "We're married," we said over and over. We ate breakfast sleepily, as though in a trance, on the veranda. My mother wanted me to take pictures to show her later: this is where I was, this is what you missed, this is where we are together.

Ballet taught me to confront limitations in my body—my back's breaking point, the height of my leg, the reality of my structure. I learned, eventually, that I must work with the body I have. Rather than focus on the physical barriers of my genes, I'd like to learn from ballet, and focus on the potential and possibility born from patience, pain, endurance, and joy. Writing was a way to heal how I'd failed in ballet, or where ballet had failed me, to inscribe my life with permanence when I know my body is as fleeting as dancing. Writing them down, like living them, lets me chance the focus of the story, as well as its ending.

17

When I was six years old, I saw an exhibit in the London Zoo about snake bites. The pictures of men throwing up blood and their skin peeling in long ribbons after getting attacked have stayed with me ever since. Like my various injuries in ballet that culminated in one final fall, my fear of snakes culminated the day I saw a snake shortly before I was sexually assaulted. For so many years I could pretend I had journeyed through that trauma. The word "rape" didn't make me flinch, nor did depictions of it in books or movies, at least not any more so than any person who is moved by human suffering. I had become a teacher and talked to college women about how to narrativize their own suffering, as though I was on the other side of my own. Admitting that I had simply transferred my trauma from one form into a new one—a snake's writhing body—let me know how much work I still had to do.

Phobias often develop in early childhood—sometimes learned by observing parents or other adults. One of my earliest memories is of Mita telling me she was terrified of snakes after seeing rattlesnakes in her yard. My mother, who inherited this fear and passed it down to me without knowing it, used to tell me not to go in tall grass where snakes might be hiding. My own ophidiophobia feels like it has always been part of me, and something I tried to hide from people to spare myself the embarrassment and frustration of explaining something that seemed ridiculous as soon as the words left my mouth.

My phobia created a lopsided dynamic in which I had to admit my utter terror to people in order to feel safe around them—if I warned them of my fear, I reasoned, they'd understand it was a forbidden topic.

⌘

The Friday night before Memorial Day weekend in 2014 was unseasonably warm, the first breaths of summer already exhaling. I was at home, far enough away from the university where I taught that I heard it on the news like the rest of the country. A young man knocked loudly on the door of Alpha Phi sorority house, and when no one answered, he opened fire on the front lawn and killed two young women. One of the young co-eds shot on the lawn, Katie Cooper, was weeks away from graduating. Her parents, seeing the news on TV, called and texted her all night. When her father used an app the next morning to track down her phone, he learned it was in the coroner's office.

On a holiday weekend, students would have either been home for the long weekend or milling around, drunk and giddy, desperate to press against each other later in the night. I wasn't there at the time, but I had been on those streets so many times, feeling secure in their familiarity. The other girl who died on the lawn of Alpha Phi, Veronika Weiss, was a freshman, a high school friend of one of my students. We have all been those two students, Friday night of a long weekend, in love with our own young bodies.

The killer began his spree by stabbing his two roommates and their friend: David Wang, James Hong, and George Chen.

They were incidental victims; James Hong had gotten in a fight with the shooter earlier that year over a measuring cup. The shooter had made a citizen's arrest and gotten his roommate in trouble.

George Chen's parents forgave the killer in an act of unimaginable magnanimity. His mother said she would die 100 times, 1,000 times, to keep her son from dying. What mother wouldn't?

During the last eight minutes of his life, the shooter drove through the streets, fatally shooting another student, Christopher Michaels-Martinez, outside the local deli. He shot and injured seven more people, and hit another seven with his black Mercedes before he crashed it. The autopsy report showed a single bullet wound through the right temple, an exit wound through the left.

I taught at the college where these students went, UC Santa Barbara, and had been an undergraduate student there some years before that night. As a student I bought my class readers for French literature in Isla Vista, where the seven students lived before they died. I went to garage band concerts, drank out of a plastic cup in a courtyard, trying to find my friends in some boy's apartment complex on a crowded Friday night. But I had always been nervous about Isla Vista—not the place so much as the people who lived there. It is a forgotten, unincorporated town that doesn't belong to the university or the city around it, and because of this seemed uniquely lawless, with absent slumlords, high crime rates, and the wreckage of a transient body of residents. They could leave soon, for the year, for the winter break, for the rest of their lives. They left their mistakes in their dry empty wake.

The morning after the mass shooting, the killer's manifesto had gone viral, in which he spelled out his plan to kill every "slut" who had ever denied him sex as "retribution" for his still being a virgin. He laughed like a cartoon villain in the videos, blaming women for his misery, and spelling out his plans to slaughter them in punishment. He thought women owed him sex, and hated them for not seeing his power and success. With a morbid fascination, I watched a YouTube video he had uploaded, looking at his face to see if he had been one of my students. His madness reflected the values around him like a fun house mirror: he was obsessed with the trappings of money and status, and placed no value in people's lives. With a chill, I recognized his sentiment, an exaggerated version of all of the men who thought I existed for their gaze when I walked down the sidewalk. Sometimes, this unwelcome gaze came from male students, whose eyes I couldn't duck. In the years since this mass shooting, the perpetrator has become a hero to the incel—or "involuntary celibate"—community online. They call him "the supreme gentleman" because he said in one of his online videos, "You girls have never been attracted to me. I don't know why you girls aren't attracted to me but I will punish you all for it. It's an injustice, a crime because I don't know what you don't see in me, I'm the perfect guy and yet you throw yourselves at all these obnoxious men instead of me, the supreme gentleman. I will punish all of you for it."

After the shooting the motto was "Isla Vista Strong," but mostly my female students were very, very scared. It's hard to explain what it feels like to grow up as prey. The story exists not in our minds, but in our bodies, the way we react to sudden noises, to being home alone, to walking through an empty parking lot long after dark.

The brush of a stranger's hand against mine can take me a full day to shake off: an arm grazing mine in a crowded space, a thigh pressed against mine in a bus seat or bench. I flinch at contact with unknown skin, sensing dangers both corporeal and intuitive. My mind wrings itself out by categorizing new definitions of touching my body: accidental, pretend accidental, forceful, violent. Some days, the best we can hope for is just to survive all the strangers who touch us.

The question is not "How do we escape from that violence?" The question is, how do women escape from being blamed for it?

⋇⊶⊷⋇

During my first appointment with Dr. Kelliher, my exposure therapist, neither of us used the word "snake" at all—we talked in euphemisms about why I was there, and what I hoped to accomplish.

"My goal is to respond to *them* like any normal person would," I told him. "Normal" sounded like a relief to me. So, with Justin's help, I began to do my first homework assignment: saying the word "calm" over and over to myself as I imagined a snake. Justin sat next to me, watching me try to take deep breaths as I practiced.

The first time Justin showed me a picture of a snake, he stood across the room so that I could barely make out the picture. He had spent years trying to protect me from what he was now showing me, from far away, on the screen of his phone.

From my safety of the couch, I couldn't make out more than the general outline of what I was looking at. I told myself, *Calm,* the direction I had taught myself to relax my whole body. The snake on the screen was barely bigger than an earthworm, curled in the palm of someone's hand. "Anxiety level is two," I reported. "You can take a step closer."

Justin had seen the exact snake on a run in the foothills of the Santa Ynez Mountains, had come home, looked it up, and waited weeks, until I was ready, to tell me about it. He stepped towards me and the snake's head, my least favorite part, came into focus. *Calm,* I told myself. "Anxiety is at a three." He took one more step towards me.

The snake was mint green and terra cotta, dwarfed by the hand in which it was coiled. "My anxiety is a four," I said. "We should stop." Any higher than a four and I was in danger of retraumatizing myself.

Dr. Kelliher had diagnosed me with PTSD.

In middle school a teacher taught us that after dark women should walk home in the middle of the street for two reasons.

The first reason I already knew, because my mother had grabbed my hand one night in London when I was six years old and pulled me into the middle of the street. "After dark, the middle of a street is safer for women," she told me. I didn't need to ask why; I had seen the news. For months, it had been covering a young mother, Rachel Nickell, who had been walking through the park with her toddler son when she was stabbed and sexually assaulted. Although it did not happen near our house, at age six I got confused and believed it happened in our local park.

I walked those paths after the case went cold, feeling the possibility of attack expanding the cathedral of my ribs. There were bad men under the canopy of every bush, caught in the dark shadows thrown by every house. As a toddler I thought Captain Hook lived behind my bed. There was never a moment I was not prepared for a man to attack me.

No one told me about the bad men who didn't hide, the ones who went to school with me, or took me on dates.

The second reason our middle school gave us for walking in the middle of the street was that otherwise no one would believe the stories we told. "If you're in the middle of the street, you might have a witness if you're attacked," she told us.

❦

The year I lived in Paris during college, I took the metro everywhere, where I could not be squeamish about bodies touching mine. Riding the train in big cities almost erases sensations of strangers' bodies pressing against each other, silently, on their way to dinner or their own homes or to meet friends in a bar, where they could laugh and argue and drink until they became sleepy. One night on my way to my friend's house, I felt a jolting motion, but it wasn't from within.

A man behind me was doing a rhythmic dance. The first thing I noticed about him was he was a businessman, dressed all in black. The second thing I noticed was his gaze, which I followed up and out the window, where we could see the graffiti etched in the glass. Then I saw what I had been too afraid to recognize: he was masturbating into my back.

I yelled in fear, telling him to stop, that he was hurting me, although he wasn't, not physically.

"Stupid bitch," he snarled back. "You are imagining things."

"I'm not," I said weakly, teary. I learned the danger of talking back to threatening men. I learned sometimes, saying nothing keeps me safe. I learned already that saying "no" to men didn't always mean they'd listen.

❦

The trauma I held was the memory of that sunny afternoon during college, and the pain I felt leaping away from that snake, with fractures in my spine, two ruptured discs leaking fluid, and a dislocated pelvis, made me feel as though, perhaps, I had died, had transcended my own body after all. It made me wonder if the assault, not the end of my ballet career, had in fact been my first death, or whether some women can survive three or four deaths during our lives if we're very lucky. My body became a memorial of these deaths—from ballet and from violence—long after I wanted to forget them.

A phobia of snakes is, apparently, the most common, but mine was worse than anyone's I'd ever met. I tried to research snakes, convinced for a time that understanding them would help me overcome my fear—a belief in "mind over matter" that I know better than to believe. But I couldn't without seeing a picture of them. Trauma isn't logical. I read even monkeys raised in labs, who have never even seen snakes, react to pictures of them.

Over the course of the Bible, from Genesis to Revelation, snakes stand in as a symbol for the devil. Like all children, the stories I heard grew my sense of the world. In my children's Bible, I carefully considered the pictures of the snake tempting Eve, the first woman on earth, long before I could read. Perhaps I was not the only child to see a parallel between my own beginnings and the beginnings of my culture. My genesis, like Eve's, began with a fall. From overhead, from grace, from safety, slipping from one identity to the next, finally crashing to the ground. What splintered, of course, was more than just a spine. It was an identity. Both are salvageable, but take constant stitching to hold in place.

❧

I had been teaching literature at UC Santa Barbara for about four years when the shooting happened. I taught in the same small college within the giant public university where I had gone as an undergrad, and the same thirty or so students appeared quarter after quarter in my classes and office to talk through reading and their writing. I loved so many of my students, many of whom half a decade later I consider good friends. After the shooting, a female student of mine said she was terrified to walk alone to class in broad daylight. Two others came to my office hours rattled after having been harassed; some were yelled at by police and college men for dressing provocatively, for not protecting themselves by covering up in the balmy days following the attacks. One young woman had PTSD from having been sexually assaulted more than once at college parties, and because of her experiences couldn't read a Faulkner novel I assigned that quarter. After the shooting, the language of grief from the campus administration was typical: a senseless tragedy, young lives taken too soon, etc. Outside my office, where student traffic in and out was steady, news cameras waited for someone willing to tell them things were going to be okay, or that things must change. The national conversations quickly turned political as advocates for gun control, and those opposed to misogyny and rape culture, used the event to illustrate their points.

The news stories focused on the killer—his Hollywood filmmaker father's offer to take him to Las Vegas to lose his virginity, how he became a "saint" for other violently misogynist misfits. What's more important about him are his actions: that after he stabbed the three young students in his own apartment, he drove to the sorority he thought had the most attractive members. He knocked on the door, but when no one answered, he opened fire. The sorority sisters who did not open the door must still hear that knocking, and they must recognize the membrane that separates them from violence.

The night after the shootings, I went to a candlelight vigil where the massacre had taken place. We walked our candles the several blocks from the campus quad past the Isla Vista Deli where Christopher Michaels-Martinez had lost his life the day before. The windows were shot out; flowers, pictures, and messages covered the ground, mourning a young man who had been in the wrong place at the wrong time. A beautiful boy, his parents' only child, had died where I was standing just hours before. He should have lived instead.

Christopher's father became a passionate advocate for stricter gun laws, because the killer walked into a gun and supply store in nearby Goleta and bought two Sig Sauer P226 semiautomatic pistols and a Glock 34 pistol, legally. The killer wrote that after he picked these up he felt a new sense of power. I wonder if the person who sold him the gun smelled someone weak and posturing, if he ever thinks about the way he could have stopped a tragedy, or if he simply felt he was doing his job.

Students came up to a microphone one-by-one to speak to the dead and to each other, and I grew restless and uncomfortable at the spectacle, but felt as though I owed it to the dead, or more so, the community who mourned them. Everything about the vigil seemed like we were looking on the bright side where there was none. One girl, who took a ballroom dancing class with Katie Cooper, said, "when I talked to you last night on the phone, I wish I would've said something, something that you would remember. I wish I would've said I love you, I wish I would've said goodbye, I wish I would've told her that her dancing was beautiful." Sometime in that last sentence the girl standing at the microphone in the night-gathered park stopped talking to the victim and began talking to the killer. But he had long ago stopped answering for himself.

Every day I am here I can reinvent my own responses to violence. I can recognize we are all beholden to fear and risk and blame, and just as beholden to the tenderness and healing we try to force so soon after tragedy. Those feelings, too, are as inevitable as nightfall.

⚜

The year before the shooting, one of my favorite students came to my office and talked around something until she couldn't keep it to herself any more. She stopped twisting her fingers and leaned forward and in the hushed voice of telling someone she has food in her teeth, finally told me. A quiet, imposing student, Joe, told a roomful of students that I wanted to sleep with him.

"No one believed him, though," she told me when she saw my agitation. "I just thought you'd want to know."

I flipped through my memories of conversations with Joe, trying to pinpoint when I might have been too nice to him, smiled at him too long, been too encouraging about his work, given him the wrong idea. The familiar feeling—of living as prey—grabbed my throat, rendering me silent. To be discussed as a sexual object rather than as a lecturer left me guessing, grasping at Joe's intentions. I wondered if it was difficult for many of my students to be taught by a young woman. That Joe said I want to sleep with him is part of a cumulative experience of womanhood, one in which men give my sexuality greater attention than they give my personhood. This fear is the backdrop of growing up female. To have my identity decided by men around me makes my very body subject to their moods and interpretation.

Fighting to uncurl our bodies from this position is lifelong work. It means defending ourselves against nothing we have said or done. It means fear of not being believed, of blowing second-hand words out of proportion, of being blamed.

I was contingent faculty, meaning subject to chance, and dependent by nature. My job existed because there was money and enrollment that year. I spent each day of my working life in a state of impermanence, depending on others to say I was worth keeping around, or worth protecting. It meant playing defense with every word and movement in my classroom, and not being able to explain why I was so tired of trying to navigate students who needed more from me than just feedback on their writing. A misstep could be ruinous.

A week or so after I learned to be afraid of Joe, he came to my office.

"I have something personal I'd like to talk to you about," he said, beginning to close the door behind him.

"Can you please leave that open?" I asked, noting how my voice changed when I was afraid and pretending not to be.

"You don't know me," he began. "You don't know my life, so I don't appreciate you passing judgments on me."

"What are you talking about?" I asked him with a calm from some hidden well of needing to survive.

"Your lectures are obviously passing judgment on my lifestyle choices." He lorded over me, blocking the open door with his body, pointing his finger in my face. I could smell his hot breath, his words slow and swimming, and I looked to the door, trying to determine whether I could slip under his arms and run outside, and whether he would chase me.

"Can you give me an example?" I asked. I knew the rolling chair between us could be a weapon if I needed it to be.

"It's obvious to everyone!" Joe shouted. I was too scared to remember to look at his hands, or his pockets, for anything that might hurt me—a gun still seemed implausible those days, since it was only abstract, conjured by a voice on the news, far away from me. A colleague heard him and looked in. I used my eyes to tell him, over Joe's shoulder, *please*. And *help*. And he understood this, through some small miracle.

"You've got to get out of here," my colleague told Joe. He was taller than Joe and surer of his words. He did not appeal to Joe's better instincts to leave me alone. He appealed to his masculinity by being bigger, by speaking louder. It was a powerful tool and one I'd never be able to brandish.

When Joe left, I sat and let myself cry quietly for about thirty seconds. My colleague stood and waited.

"I'm fine," I told him. "He didn't even touch me. He just scared me."

Ten minutes later I walked into my next class and saw Joe sitting in the back, silent, looking at his desk. I shuffled papers around, asked students some questions about the reading, looked at the clock often, and cast my gaze toward the door and the window to see if they were open. During that class, I did not feel like a teacher; I only felt like a woman, a body in danger. I let my students talk about Djuna Barnes while Joe sat against a wall, arms folded across his chest, and I was careful what I said about the Lost Generation writers, aware that Joe apparently thought any reference to them— their writing, their sexuality—was a coded message, a judgment of him. Once I saw that the sun was slanting through the blinds into his eyes; without stopping my lecture, I walked over and lowered the blinds, shading his eyes from the sun. Appeasing him felt like a way to keep myself safe.

After class I went to the front office to ask what I should do. One of the older professors in my department had told me the best way to job security was to slip under the radar. "Don't draw attention to yourself," he told me.

"Did he touch you?" the woman at the front desk asked when I told her what happened.

"No," I said. *Not exactly. Not with his hands. There are lots of ways to be touched*, is what I wish I had said. But I didn't, because I wanted to keep my credibility and my job.

The mental acrobatics I did to figure out my own responsibility reminded me so much of being nineteen and explaining away how what had happened to me could not be called rape.

That is why I got the phone number for distressed students and called to ask for a wellness check for Joe, pretending I was concerned about his safety rather than my own. That is how I slipped into adjunct personhood—by being quiet, by not drawing attention to myself, by ignoring my own instincts so fully that I do not recognize the self that did it.

I did file a campus-wide restraining order, which meant Joe could no longer take my classes. I looked the other way when I saw him in the halls. It was the smallest means of protection, but I clutched it like a shield and tried not to feel sorry I had done it, or histrionic because he never actually touched me.

The shooting threw my close call with Joe into relief, reminding me of the veil separating me from danger. After the Isla Vista shooting, I worried I was one of the people Joe would come for first if he ever snapped. I worried that by choosing my job over my life, it might be possible to lose both.

Joe felt blamed, victimized, scared, and alone, just like the shooter. Joe, too, later wrote a manifesto and posted it online, one in which he claimed the FBI was trying to pin the Isla Vista murders on him and Amnesty International was not returning his calls. When I saw this, I felt both relieved that I had not imagined the full danger Joe could have posed, and guilty for not making a bigger deal out of his threat. Sometimes we think we're over something and then act the same way again, so many years later. The relationship between Joe and the real shooter was not only in my mind—he had made that connection as well. Perhaps his permanence also felt contingent on being believed.

My own body hangs in the balance, as does the choice I make as a woman each time I worry about believability, permanence, and the roll of the dice each day. In crowded rooms, I look for Exit signs. Once, I led students in a Q&A with Zadie Smith, who was visiting the university as part of a lecture tour. When someone dropped a metal water bottle on the concrete floor, we all ducked. "I thought it was a gun," Zadie Smith said. Of course, I had thought the exact same thing. I always think the same thing when I hear a loud noise in public. Decisions I make since the shooting near my work are based ón instinct, the fear of violence stored in my bones as surely as the pain in my spine. I think about the bounty of life as often as I remember its fragility. If life were not fragile, we would not protect it so.

⚜

Every story is about my body, I realized years later. And every story is about the time my body was not my own, but a man's. It's a small story in many ways—it's duration as an event, the amount of time I think about it now—but it has a way of taking over when I tell it.

I had learned, too, in ballet my body was not my own—it belonged to the audience, to my male partner, to the choreographer who told it what to do and how.

And like with the Isla Vista shooter, and like with the pain in my back, names are not important. I don't want to name the shooter, although his name is easy to find online. I don't much want to name the person who held me down one afternoon and raped me while I lay crying on a bed. I said "no" once, and only once. And after that I left my own body and took flight and went to my mother's lap until it was over. Then, there was lots of blood.

People respond to violence differently. After my rape, I didn't let anyone kiss me for five years. I'm still jumpy, but eventually learned to feel safe in my own skin. The shooter taught me I never really could.

My life, perhaps like the lives of all or most women, has been punctuated by the violence of girl- and womanhood, which once paralyzed me into a sort of stunned silence. But knowing my silence was expected made me want to use my voice the more—I'd spent so much time trying to forget the quiet, acquiescent ballerina I'd wanted to be. And by now I was getting it, that the silence of victims of violence leaves too much room for the voices of others. To fill the space, I had to practice using my voice and telling the truth. Writing has allowed a new voice to emerge, the kind that reports crimes and demands justice. "If our voices are essential aspects of our humanity," writes Rebecca Solnit in *The Mother of All Questions*, "to be rendered voiceless is to be dehumanized or excluded from one's humanity. And the history of silence is central to women's history." Because writing gave me the voice I felt robbed of in ballet, I wrote things down as soon as they happened, no longer forced to cobble together my memories to find meaning. My voice, after all, gave me recourse. I could name the distinct power of saying "no." And "enough."

⁂

Snakes have between 200 and 400 vertebrae, while humans have only 33—snakes are more bones than we are. My own vertebrae have given shape to my body as well as the story I tell about it, of ballet and falling, not from grace, like Eve, but perhaps to grace, to a journey of deliverance. Like others who fear snakes, I am fixated on how they move, ever a dancer.

For most people, as soon as an immediate threat stops, the nervous system begins restoring our usual hormone levels, and the brain shifts back to normal. Our rational brain, the part that tells us, for example, a snake is not poisonous, kicks in.

When I saw a snake, my limbic system increased stress hormones and I reacted through either flight or freezing. The shift from reacting to responding never happened. I was still reacting to the first snake I ever saw, over a decade before my therapy, that I associated with not being in control of my own safety or body, freefalling, of saying no to someone who didn't listen.

"You associated snakes with this feeling of danger," Dr. Kelliher told me. "If you had seen someone walking by with pink hair, you might have been afraid of pink hair instead."

Half the time, instead of talking about snakes, I sat with Dr. Kelliher and talked about all the men who had made me feel unsafe, and how even when our interactions came to nothing, I had felt lucky to escape.

"Not all snakes bite," Dr. Kelliher reminded me. Snakes are not a perfect metaphor for the threats around us every day, but they're what I have. In fact, snakes don't bite unless someone interacts with them, one thing I knew I had control over. And what I told Dr. Kelliher was that it was hard to know when encountering a snake which ones would bite, and which ones would retreat. But he pointed out snakes were different from the violence I was trying to understand. My position in the world taught me to second-guess who might want to hurt me—the well-meaning dance partner, the ex-boyfriend, the angry student—and how to move out of their paths. I'd like to say I spot them sooner now, that I see them moving in the grass and step around them, but this is a life's work, and one that requires vigilance as much as it requires faith.

The day my mother took me to the Natural History Museum, where there was a stuffed snake whose tail rattled when we pushed a button, I felt such pride in myself. After that, Dr. Kelliher asked me what it was I thought I couldn't escape from. He asked me if there was a difference between the snake in the cage and the snake in the path, perceived risks and real risks. It took me a long time to learn to say yes. That it was possible to escape from a snake but not from real violence.

❧

Recently, as I wrote this chapter, I received an eight-paragraph Facebook message from Joe, as though writing about him eerily invoked him. "So apparently Your Daddy tried to get me murdered with a soundbyte," he wrote. "He intentionally misinterpreted Othello and Chaucer's *Canterbury Tales* in order to manipulate everyone into thinking I'm an asshole." My father had been one of his professors too. Joe wrote that the university and all his professors had exploited his schizophrenia, murdered his parents, and abandoned him.

This time, I picked up the phone and called the police.

Officer Power guessed the student's name before I'd even finished the story, and said he'd add it to Joe's file. "We consider him an empty threat," he told me. Joe was now homeless, he explained, confined to a three-mile radius on his bike, without a cell phone or any other means of transportation. "He doesn't want any treatment," the police officer told me. "He just wants people to hear him. There are two hundred miles between you—the worst that might happen is an angry internet comment."

Rather than reassuring me, it scared me to learn the exact distance between Joe and me. It wasn't enough. But by speaking up and writing it down, I felt that this time I had claimed my own body and the voice it contains. And now that Justin was with me, his sympathy comforted me, even as it could not save me. I had been believed. I could name the ways in which my life is not wholly contingent on what someone else says or does.

⚜

A year after my first appointment, I was ready for the pet store. It took me a few months of walking towards the reptile section before I got all the way up to the glass cage, but Justin told me the ball python was lethargic and docile. "Think of it as the golden retriever of snakes," he said.

Eventually I made it all the way up to the cage and looked in, while Justin rubbed my back and told me I was doing a great job and I felt like a child but also proud. In front of anyone else I would've been embarrassed to celebrate such a small victory, but Justin knew what a defining moment this was, and how free I felt as this phobia loosened its grip over me.

"You don't rely on anyone for your safety," Dr. Kelliher told me towards the end of exposure therapy. "You can be safe by yourself." I should have known this was coming next, that once again, a man couldn't save me. I should have known what it means to save myself since I have done it over and over again.

What I didn't realize about exposure therapy is that I'd eventually have to face the snake alone, just the two of us, face-to-beady-eyed-face.

Dr. Kelliher was a mountaineer, and used metaphors related to the way he saw the world—"you can change your own summit," he once told me when I changed my final goal from seeing a snake to touching one. "You don't have to like it," he said. "You just have to know you can do it."

The first time I went in to the pet store alone I could only make it to the dog treat bar before I turned around and left. The next time, I made it all the way to the birdcage, where I looked through the bars to the snakes. Eventually I made it to the snake cage but looked at them through my phone screen, separated from the animals right in front of me by the small-scale reproduction of them. Once, I touched the glass of the cage, and the snake pressed its body back against my finger on the other side of the glass. And eventually, I made it all the way up to the glass, took a deep breath to remind myself I was safe, and looked in the cage. I took a selfie with the snake and sent it to Justin. "Phobia is ancient hisssssstory!" I texted.

Like in ballet, I had lost my audience, and without the performance of healing, I could focus on really getting over this great boulder in my path.

The final step came without any planning, which meant I didn't have to worry about it all morning. One Saturday morning, Justin and I went to our local natural history museum, something we had never done before. We walked around oak-shaded paths by a creek and Justin told me it was too cold for snakes, something he had gotten used to telling me. On one of the paths was a white tent with a woman, sitting on a stool, next to a snake in a cage. Justin was not used to me wanting to watch the snake, something I liked to do to challenge myself, to let myself bask in what I was capable of doing.

"Would you like me to take it out of the cage?" the woman asked me. I told her my relationship to snakes, and said, yes, I was ready, but I'd go far away from her and come as close as I could.

The woman sat in a patch of sunlight with the gopher snake in her hands, and let him curl around her wrists and neck. "You're in a good mood today, aren't you?" she asked him. I walked up close to her and watched the snake and felt how tense I was. *Calm*, I told myself, and unclenched.

A little boy walked up to the woman and asked if he could pet the snake. His mother was behind us with another child, perhaps afraid of the snake herself.

"Show me your petting fingers," the woman holding the snake said to the little boy. She held up two fingers on her right hand and the boy did the same. "We pet towards the tail, like a kitten," she told him, and showed him the right way. He leaned down and gently petted the snake as it moved up the woman's arm.

I turned to Justin. "I'm going to do it," I said. I felt electric, plugged in. He stood behind me and I leaned over and touched that goddamned snake, knowing nothing could happen to me, knowing I was safe, and I could leave any time I wanted. As soon as my fingers made contact, I shouted and jumped back, scaring the little boy a little, I think, so I turned to him and told him how nice that snake was so he wouldn't learn to be afraid like I was. On the way back to the car I held my petting fingers in my lap until I could wash my hands, knowing I had done it, I had touched the snake. I had done more than survive.

Two days later, I graduated from exposure therapy.

⚬⚬⚬

What happened in Isla Vista affected me in all the roles I played. I chose my job over my physical safety, a decision that felt like the easiest way to disappear into safety. And choosing my job is a form of safety as well—financial security that allows me to provide for myself, to avoid being contingent in other ways, dependent on my family or husband. Maybe being human means depending on someone for some form of safety, the precarious state in which we all find ourselves. It might mean there can never be such thing as safety from the very forces that threaten us, although there are so many ways we pretend we are, and so many times we put ourselves in each other's hands and still survive. I think about this more often than I'd like to admit—each time I'm a passenger and Justin drives, for example. Or when I trust the doctors, years later, who find cancer in my mother's left breast and remove it through so many violent means. I think about it when I remember my ballet partner dropping me when I trusted him, how that fact changed the illusion of safety I lived beneath, and made me grateful to learn that trust builds up again. It has to, or else none of us would ever go outside.

There are just as many stories within a single event as there are selves to read them. What happened in Isla Vista affects me as a teacher, as a former student, as a woman who has experienced sexual assault at the hands of someone who felt entitled to her body. In the days after the mass shooting, I was struck by how much I recognized the feelings of the killer, and how scared I was of that sympathy. I have felt rejection, loneliness, frustration. The truth of that ripples outwards in small currents, whirling in all directions. It is empathy in the face of violence, and I'm just as proud of this as I am afraid of it. What I did not recognize was his response to those feelings.

Some of us learn how to hold these stories in our bodies in one violent rush, and some learn gradually, muscle by muscle, over time. It's nothing but survival. Every woman who survives will have to keep surviving for the rest of her life, holding herself safe, holding her own story so it's not dismissed, erased, written over by someone with a louder voice. Every woman who tells her story of survival will be telling a story of victory.

The silence of victims of violence is the silence of women who have been told their stories aren't believable. When I was nineteen, I refused my own voice, thinking it was too quiet, but as an adult, I feel fully charged. Using my voice feels like assertion, activism, consent in the stories in which I participated. Using my voice liberates me, and when there isn't a place for the story I wanted to tell, I write it down instead.

❧

I wrote I was healed from this phobia, and it became true.

"Will you add it to your book?" Dr. Kelliher asked me during our last session.

"I think I did it so I could finish my book."

"Or you used the book as an excuse to face the snake," he suggested. I felt the truth of this statement fall on me like dawn.

"I should have done this all sooner," I told him. "I wasted so many years being afraid."

"You can't climb if you don't have oxygen," he said. None of us can touch the snake, or face our tormentor, until the moment we are ready, our bodies and amygdalas relaxed, until we find our escape routes and don't have to use them.

"I'll see you out there on the hiking trails," he said, as we said goodbye at our final session. And Justin and I kept an eye out on those trails, both for Dr. Kelliher and for snakes. But by then, I could also look around and enjoy the scenery.

Later in the year, I saw my first snake in the wild, a king snake, just like the first one I ever saw. I was with Justin and his brother's family, who were visiting us for the week. We were on our way to the beach when Justin called out and looked back at me. I said "Oh my god" twice as I watched the snake make its way across our path. And once it was out of our way, we kept walking, and had a lovely day at the beach.

"I'm going to buy you a pair of snakeskin boots to celebrate how well you handled that," Justin said that evening. I didn't want to wear snakeskin on my feet, but I don't think I've ever been prouder of anything than I was of how calmly I observed the snake in our path. It didn't want to hurt me after all.

Since I finished exposure therapy, I try harder to be kinder to my body, to battle for its autonomy and life on its own terms. Like the nerves and bones that compose us, our minds have their own muscle memory. In fighting for our lives, in flight or when freezing—our muscle memories make us elastic and steadfast, attuned to the delicate dance between safety and surrender, between falling and dancing.

Like so much of life, hard work takes place offstage. I've learned to brace my own mind and heart as an adult just as I learned to brace my own body as a teenager. I used to think just naming my fear was courageous. But I realized that trying to heal was even braver. It was never the fear that defined me. It was my resolve to face it that showed who I am. Phobias and their treatment are a series of building up and breaking down defenses, of trying and failing and trying again. The same could be said of love.

I'm learning to shift from reaction to response, to run away and scream or to remain and face things. I am relearning what it means to feel safe in the world, and in my own skin, letting fear and grief go back to sleep until the next time they are awakened. But then I will recall all the times I've put them to bed so far, and let those guide the times I will do it all over again.

My body, a site of pain and trauma, and ultimately, healing, my harbor of love. Snakes, too, a source of terror, were not the thing itself, but a representation of some other truth. The truth can be transformed.

Now, I say *Calm* to myself, meaning I am here, meaning I have the resources to take care of myself, meaning I have had those all along.

Acknowledgments

Thank you first and foremost to Katie Grimm, more than an agent, who pulled this book out of me, and who has been on my team since the beginning. This book wouldn't exist without her. She believed in it so much she once called me from the hospital to give me a pep talk.

Thank you to Melville House, who ushered my writing to its final form. To Michael Barron, who first advocated for me. To Kirsten Reach, who moved the puzzle pieces into place with intelligence and such kindness, and to Athena Bryan, the editor of my dreams, who polished this until it shone, and who celebrated each small victory alongside me. Thank you also to Cassie Gutman for your thoughtful copyediting and to Valerie Merians for all you have done behind the curtain.